MANHOOD
God's Style

Rev. Wilbur Conway

© Copyright 1999 — Wilbur Conway

All rights reserved. This book is protected under the copyright laws of the United States of America. This book may not be copied or reprinted for commercial gain or profit. The use of short quotations or occasional page copying for personal or group study is permitted and encouraged. Permission will be granted upon request. Unless otherwise identified, Scripture quotations are from the King James Version of the Bible. Scriptures marked NKJ are from the New King James Version of the Bible. Please note that Destiny Image's publishing style capitalizes certain pronouns in Scripture that refer to the Father, Son, and Holy Spirit, and may differ from some Bible publishers' styles. Emphasis in Scripture is the author's own.

Take note that the name satan and related names are not capitalized. We choose not to acknowledge him, even to the point of violating grammatical rules.

Treasure House
An Imprint of
Destiny Image® Publishers, Inc.
P.O. Box 310
Shippensburg, PA 17257-0310

"For where your treasure is,
there will your heart be also." Matthew 6:21

ISBN 1-56043-318-3

For Worldwide Distribution
Printed in the U.S.A.

This book and all other Destiny Image, Revival Press,
and Treasure House books are available
at Christian bookstores and distributors worldwide.

For a U.S. bookstore nearest you, call **1-800-722-6774**.
For more information on foreign distributors, call **717-532-3040**.
Or reach us on the Internet: **http://www.reapernet.com**

Dedication

To Corinne, my wife of 40 years; to my four daughters, Karen, Janine, Sandra, and Robin; and to my five grandchildren, Orlance, Mark, John, Kimberly, and Pearl.

Thanks to Stephen W. Nance, Elizabeth C. Allen, and the staff of Destiny Image for their assistance and support.

Contents

Part One	**Where Are All the Men?**	1
Chapter One	Will the Real Men Please Stand Up?	3
Chapter Two	Men of the World	11
Chapter Three	Despising the Birthright	19
Part Two	**God's Plan for Men**	27
Chapter Four	Priest	29
Chapter Five	Provider	39
Chapter Six	Protector	45
Part Three	**"Styling" God**	53
Chapter Seven	Jesus, Our Example of Manhood	55
Chapter Eight	Fruit of the Spirit	65
Chapter Nine	Men of God	73
Part Four	**Rise Up, O Men of God**	81
Chapter Ten	Rise Up in the Home	83
Chapter Eleven	Rise Up in the Church	91
Chapter Twelve	Rise Up in the Community	99

Part One

Where Are All the Men?

Most men will proclaim every one his own goodness: but a faithful man who can find? (Proverbs 20:6)

Chapter One

Will the Real Men Please Stand Up?

For if a man think himself to be something, when he is nothing, he deceiveth himself (Galatians 6:3).

Styling. People do it everywhere: along inner-city streets; among urban gangs; in suburban neighborhoods; in schools, churches, factories, and offices; in big cities and in small towns. In some way or another, all of us "style." I do it, and so do you. Styling is in the way we talk, the way we act, the way we dress. Our speech, our behavior, and our attire all reflect where we have come from, whom we admire, and what we think of ourselves.

Whether it's a sports figure, a movie star, an entertainer, some other icon of the popular culture, or even a religious leader—everybody styles somebody. When word got out that Michael Jordan had his shirts custom-made by a certain tailor in Memphis, Tennessee, it seemed as if every Michael Jordan fan wanted shirts made by that same tailor. They were "styling" Michael Jordan.

Although styling is not gender-specific—both men and women do it—my focus in this book is on men. We might as well admit it, guys, we style as much as anybody. Sometimes it is conscious, sometimes not. If I put on a new outfit and go stand on the street corner, and the rest of the guys show up, they might say that I was "styling" this suit, or "styling" my new shoes. Over recent years male "styling" has shown up in many different ways. Today, it's the earring in one ear, a baseball cap worn backward, or pants worn below the waistline. A few years ago it was the athletic shoes worn without tying the laces. During the 1980's "styling" in the corporate world was the IBM "power suit": a black or dark blue suit, a white shirt, and a red– or blue–striped tie.

Whatever form it takes, styling is part of our attempt at self-identity; an expression of how we see ourselves and how we want others to see us. It is a way of drawing attention to ourselves and saying to the world, "This is who I am." The problem is that far too many men today don't *know* who they are. Our culture has encouraged many false and inaccurate ideas of true manhood, with the result that entire generations of males are growing up confused and ignorant of what it means to be a man.

We need a clear and constant standard of true manhood for us to measure ourselves against. Fortunately, we have one. Genesis 1:27 says, "So God created man in His own image, in the image of God created He him; male and female created He them." Since God created man in His own image and likeness, what better "style" could we have? It's not Michael Jordan or Michael Jackson, Bill Clinton or even Billy Graham. As men, we need to learn to style ourselves after *God*.

In the beginning, Adam "styled" God perfectly, just as he had been created to do. He knew who he was and what his relationship was to God and to Eve, who was created to be his companion and helpmeet. His sin came when through disobedience to God he tried to "style" himself as higher and mightier than he really was, as someone who didn't need to be under God's authority. He gave up his created place as a man "after God's style" for that of a man "after the devil's style." With Adam, "styling" God was lost, and men have struggled to get it back ever since.

Many men today suffer from identity problems. Knowing neither themselves nor God's style of manhood, they take on the false styles of the world in an attempt to identify themselves as men. These styles, of which there are many, are reflected in their words, behavior, and lifestyle. The three that follow are among the most common and are representative of all the false images of manhood that males have picked up from the world:

1. "I can do it myself. I don't need anyone else."

One false image many males have of manhood is that a real man is a loner who neither needs nor asks for help from anyone. He is tough as nails, never shows any weakness, and never cries. Such a "man" is totally self-sufficient in all areas of life; he needs nothing from anyone, including God. He values no opinions except his own. Whatever he can't get through intimidation or sheer determination of will, he may take by force or violence. The theme of his life is expressed by the song made famous by the late Frank Sinatra, "I Did It My Way." The women and children in his life often are considered more as objects for domination and control than as people to be loved and nurtured.

There's nothing "manly" about this "Lone Ranger" mentality (besides, even the Lone Ranger had help: Tonto). If God is our standard, then His Word is our guide, and the Bible makes it clear that "going it alone" has nothing to do with true manhood. True men recognize their need for the presence of God as well as the fellowship and help of other people.

Moses is a good example. This great man of God knew that he needed the constant presence and power of God with him or he could do nothing:

> *Then Moses said to the Lord, "See, You say to me, 'Bring up this people.' But You have not let me know whom You will send with me. Yet You have said, 'I know you by name, and you have also found grace in My sight.' Now therefore, I pray, if I have found grace in Your sight, show me now Your way, that I may know You and that I may find*

grace in Your sight. And consider that this nation is Your people." And He said, "My Presence will go with you, and I will give you rest." Then he said to Him, "If Your Presence does not go with us, do not bring us up from here" (Exodus 33:12-15 NKJ).

Moses needed human assistance, too. When Israel fought with Amalek, Moses stood on a hill watching the battle. Whenever he raised his arms, Israel prevailed; when he lowered his arms, Amalek prevailed. As Moses grew tired, Aaron and Hur stood on either side of him, holding his arms up so that Israel defeated Amalek (see Ex. 17:10-13). In the very next chapter, Moses heeded the advice of his father-in-law, Jethro, and appointed other men as leaders among the Israelites to assist him in instructing the people (see Ex. 18:13-27).

Real men acknowledge their need for others. The writer of Ecclesiastes says:

Two are better than one; because they have a good reward for their labour. For if they fall, the one will lift up his fellow: but woe to him that is alone when he falleth; for he hath not another to help him up. Again, if two lie together, then they have heat: but how can one be warm alone? And if one prevail against him, two shall withstand him; and a threefold cord is not quickly broken (Ecclesiastes 4:9-12).

Another example is Jesus Himself. He chose 12 men to be His special friends, companions, and disciples whom He would commission to continue His work. Just hours before His crucifixion, when He entered the Garden of Gethsemane to pray, He felt the need for the presence and support of Peter, James, and John, His three closest friends among the disciples (see Mt. 26:37-46). If Jesus knew the need for help from others, then who are we, any of us, to claim that we can go it alone?

Indeed, Jesus expressed the reality quite well when He said, "I am the vine, ye are the branches: He that abideth in Me, and I in him, the same bringeth forth much fruit: for *without Me ye can do nothing*" (Jn. 15:5).

Real men realize that true manhood does not mean going it alone. Real men have the courage and integrity to acknowledge the need for God and for others in their lives!

2. "What I do is no one else's business."

A common attitude, which pervades much of our culture, says that our behavior as individuals affects no one but ourselves and therefore should be of no concern to anyone else. It is the "You mind your own business and I'll mind mine" syndrome. The fallacy of this mindset should be obvious: Only hermits live in isolation. Our behavior *does* affect others. When your behavior affects *me*, it *becomes* my business.

Many men today live by this philosophy. They do whatever they want, whenever they want, to whomever they want, with little or no concern over the consequences of their actions. One result is the nationwide disgrace that millions of single mothers across this nation are struggling to raise fatherless children: fractured families abandoned by males who were "male" enough to father children but not "man" enough to shoulder the responsibilities that go with it.

Men who live this way say by their actions, "I will do as I please, accountable to no one, responsible to no one except myself." Such an attitude is based on a distorted view of personal freedom fueled by selfishness, which has its root in pride, the original sin of Adam in the garden of Eden. The Bible is quite plain concerning the error of this kind of thinking:

> *The way of a fool is right in his own eyes: but he that hearkeneth unto counsel is wise* (Proverbs 12:15).

> *There is a way which seemeth right unto a man; but the end thereof are the ways of death* (Proverbs 14:12).

> *All the ways of a man are clean in his own eyes; but the Lord weigheth the spirits* (Proverbs 16:2).

The Word of God says that a man who listens only to his own voice is a *fool*. He who justifies his own actions by nothing more than his own counsel is headed down a path that leads to death. What we think about ourselves is not nearly as important as what God thinks. He sees into our hearts, into the very core of our being.

One quality of *true* manhood, manhood God's style, is a sensitive concern for the effect and influence that our personal behavior has on other people. Styling God means reflecting His image, heart, and nature in us, which involves placing a greater importance on the needs and welfare of others than on our personal rights and desires. The apostle Paul illustrated this when he wrote to the church at Corinth:

> *But take heed lest by any means this liberty of yours become a stumblingblock to them that are weak. For if any man see thee which hast knowledge sit at meat in the idol's temple, shall not the conscience of him which is weak be emboldened to eat those things which are offered to idols; and through thy knowledge shall the weak brother perish, for whom Christ died? But when ye sin so against the brethren, and wound their weak conscience, ye sin against Christ. Wherefore, if meat make my brother to offend, I will eat no flesh while the world standeth, lest I make my brother to offend* (1 Corinthians 8:9-13).

As believers, we have freedom in Christ, but that does not give us the right to live without regard for the effect that our behavior has on others. True manhood means being willing to restrain our personal liberty and actions for the greater good of others.

Real men realize that true manhood involves living with a sensitive regard for the dignity and worth of other people and an unselfish concern for their welfare.

3. "And yes, by the way, I am superior to all others."

Although few of us would admit it outright, most of us men tend to think pretty highly of ourselves. We are more "macho" than anybody else, or the best lover, or better skilled and qualified than any of our coworkers, and we're *always* smarter than our boss! This is the pride of Eden, the seed of the rebellion against God that was Adam's downfall. I'm not talking about the positive pride in hard-earned accomplishments or knowledge of a job well done, or honest recognition of one's gifts and abilities. I'm talking about the deadly pride of elevating ourselves in our own minds above other people, lifting ourselves above our proper place in relation to God, and generally having a higher regard for ourselves than we should.

Because such pride was the ruin of man in Eden, it should be no surprise that the Bible is full of warnings against it:

Pride goeth before destruction, and an haughty spirit before a fall (Proverbs 16:18).

It is not good to eat much honey: so for men to search their own glory is not glory (Proverbs 25:27).

Thus saith the Lord, Let not the wise man glory in his wisdom, neither let the mighty man glory in his might, let not the rich man glory in his riches: But let him that glorieth glory in this, that he understandeth and knoweth Me, that I am the Lord which exercise lovingkindness, judgment, and righteousness, in the earth: for in these things I delight, saith the Lord (Jeremiah 9:23-24).

For I say, through the grace given unto me, to every man that is among you, not to think of himself more highly than he ought to think; but to think soberly, according as God hath dealt to every man the measure of faith (Romans 12:3).

The entire fourth chapter of the Book of Daniel is devoted to the account of how God humbled a proud king. Nebuchadnezzar, king of Babylon, credited himself for the power, might, and wisdom of his kingdom. His heart was lifted up in pride, and God afflicted him with madness for a time. He was driven from the presence of men and lived with the animals of the field, even eating the grass of the field as the animals did. After seven years, his reason returned, and he humbled himself before God. Restored to his throne, a wiser and meeker king declared, "Now I Nebuchadnezzar praise and extol and honour the King of heaven, all whose works are truth, and His ways judgment: and those that walk in pride He is able to abase" (Dan. 4:37).

Jesus told a parable that sharply contrasts the deadly nature of pride with the redemptive quality of humility:

And He spake this parable unto certain which trusted in themselves that they were righteous, and despised others: Two men went up into the temple to pray; the one a Pharisee, and the other a publican. The Pharisee stood and prayed thus with himself, God, I thank Thee, that I am not as other men are, extortioners, unjust, adulterers, or even as this publican. I fast twice in the week, I give tithes of all that I possess. And the publican, standing afar off, would not lift up so much as his eyes unto heaven, but smote upon his breast, saying, God be merciful to me a sinner. I tell you, this man went down to his house justified rather than the other: for every one that exalteth himself shall be abased; and he that humbleth himself shall be exalted (Luke 18:9-14).

Pride blinded the Pharisee to his spiritual need and kept him completely cut off from God. The publican, on the other hand, acknowledged his sin and, in humility, sought God's mercy. His humble repentance brought access to God's grace, and he went home justified. Jesus' warning is stark: The proud will be humbled, but the humble will be lifted up. Pride is deadly and has nothing whatsoever to do with manhood.

Real men realize that true manhood involves a humble spirit toward God and a sober, down-to-earth assessment of themselves.

Chapter Two

Men of the World

Love not the world, neither the things that are in the world. If any man love the world, the love of the Father is not in him. For all that is in the world, the lust of the flesh, and the lust of the eyes, and the pride of life, is not of the Father, but is of the world (1 John 2:15-16).

There seems to be a shortage of men in every segment of our society. Oh, there are plenty of *males* running around, but true men—*God-style men*—are hard to find. Across our land, millions of children are growing up without a stable, positive manly role model in their lives. In these homes, the man is either absent entirely, or, if present, he sends confusing and contradictory messages often characterized by irresponsibility, abuse and immaturity. Many single mothers are working hard against great obstacles and with no male support to raise their children responsibly, and many are succeeding. They are to be commended. The problem is, they should not *have to* do it alone. Children have a much better chance of becoming mature, well-adjusted adults when they grow up under the influence of clear role models from *both* a mother *and* a father. Where are the men who will *love* their wives, be *fathers* to their children and "bring them up in the nurture and admonition of the Lord" (see Eph. 6:4)?

This shortage of men is a problem even within the Church, the Body of Christ. In my travels I am hearing from many of my sisters in Christ that many single women who desire to marry are frustrated by the lack of marriageable men in our churches. The men who are available, they say, seem uninterested in long-term relationships. Many of our churches also have trouble finding enough committed, qualified men to provide leadership as deacons, elders, teachers, and other important positions of influence. Where are the men who will stand up and be counted for Christ, serving Him faithfully and inspiring future generations of godly church leaders?

Men are at a premium in many areas of the wider community as well. Public education is a good example. In the elementary grades, where children's values and self-images are still in the formative stages, male career teachers are scarce. It is possible in many of our school systems today for a boy to progress from the first grade through high school graduation with only one or two men teachers, and those are usually coaches. For the most part, the burden of instructing and caring for the children in our society is borne by women: teachers, day-care providers, counselors, social workers, etc. Our women can't do the job alone, nor should they have to. For the sake of our children, we men also need to place ourselves in *every* segment of our society. Where are the men who will commit themselves to be positive moral, spiritual, and ethical role models for the children and youth in their communities?

Why is there such a scarcity of God-style manhood in our culture today? I believe it is because humanity has drifted so far from God's original design and ideal that many people, both men and women, have no clue as to what their identities and roles are as men and women. Paul described to Timothy the attitudes of those who did not know God. What was true in their day is true in ours:

> *But know this, that in the last days perilous times will come: For men will be lovers of themselves, lovers of money, boasters, proud, blasphemers, disobedient to parents, unthankful, unholy, unloving, unforgiving, slanderers, without self-control, brutal, despisers of good, traitors, headstrong, haughty, lovers of pleasures rather than lovers of God, having a form of godliness but denying its power. And from such people turn away!* (2 Timothy 3:1-5 NKJ)

In short, the lack of men is the work of satan. Sinful activity of all kinds has robbed our society of its men. Many are in penal institutions or hanging out on the street corners. A growing number are falling prey to homosexuality and becoming decimated by AIDS. Many men refuse to look to God for answers, or even to acknowledge God. Whatever form it takes, this sinfulness can be catalogued somewhere under the three "p's" of *pride, prosperity,* or *perversion.*

Pride

An Old Testament proverb describes today's generation so well that it could have been written yesterday:

> *There is a generation that are pure in their own eyes, and yet is not washed from their filthiness. There is a generation, O how lofty are their eyes! And their eyelids are lifted up* (Proverbs 30:12-13).

Pride is a significant factor in explaining the attitudes and behavior of "men of the world." Many men truly believe that they are in charge of their lives and refuse to take instruction from anyone else. In their pride they make wrong choices, often because of the lack of counsel or their failure to heed good advice. Our society encourages men to be completely independent and self-sufficient. This is contrary to the counsel of Scripture, where God says it is important for all mankind to look to and depend on Him:

Trust in the Lord with all thine heart; and lean not unto thine own understanding. In all thy ways acknowledge Him, and He shall direct thy paths (Proverbs 3:5-6).

God created us to be totally dependent upon Him, and only in that relationship do we find security. Therein lies another problem with pride.

For countless men, pride is a mask they use to cover up their insecurities. Cut off from God and not knowing what to do or who to turn to, they are unsure of themselves, their place in the world, and their relationships with others. Proud men rarely, if ever, ask for help in resolving negative situations they find themselves in. Seeking to justify their insecurities, they blame God, their parents, their spouses, their supervisors—anyone except themselves—for their inadequacies.

Men also use pride to disguise their fear. Our worldly culture teaches that fear is a weakness, and no man wants to be thought of as a weakling. So fear and pride become snares that prevent men from fulfilling the role and purpose God has for them. The Book of Proverbs says, "The fear of man bringeth a snare: but whoso putteth his trust in the Lord shall be safe" (Prov. 29:25).

Insecurity, fear, and feelings of inferiority drive many men to seek escape or fulfillment in sex, alcohol, drugs, or other addictive and self-destructive habits. Their main focus in life becomes the pleasing of self, and selfishness is the central core of pride. Pride is sin. Sin hinders faith. Without faith it is impossible to please God (see Heb. 11:6), and only by pleasing God can men truly please themselves and others.

Prosperity

The apostle Paul wrote to Timothy that worldly men were "lovers of money" (2 Tim. 3:1-2 NKJ), and that "the love of money is the root of all evil" (1 Tim. 6:10). Love of money and the quest for material prosperity drive much of our modern society. Acquisition of wealth is presented as the primary goal of life. We are surrounded by "get-rich-quick" schemes of every kind.

Men of the World

Nationwide, millions play the lottery, the horses, and the casinos. Anything that men can bet on, they do. The lure of quick, easy money draws many men into drug-dealing and other kinds of criminal activity. The pull of prosperity is everywhere. Even some parts of the Church preach a prosperity message.

Now don't misunderstand me. There is nothing wrong with money or prosperity of themselves. The *love* of money is the problem. Scripture never condemns prosperity, but it warns repeatedly of the danger of letting its pursuit become the consuming obsession of life. Jesus said, "No man can serve two masters: for either he will hate the one, and love the other; or else he will hold to the one, and despise the other. Ye cannot serve God and mammon" (Mt. 6:24). Many people today have fallen into precisely that trap: mammon *is* their god. Matthew records a sobering example of this:

> *And, behold, one came and said unto Him, Good Master, what good thing shall I do, that I may have eternal life? And He said unto him, Why callest thou Me good? there is none good but one, that is, God: but if thou wilt enter into life, keep the commandments. He saith unto Him, Which? Jesus said, Thou shalt do no murder, Thou shalt not commit adultery, Thou shalt not steal, Thou shalt not bear false witness, Honour thy father and thy mother: and, Thou shalt love thy neighbour as thyself. The young man saith unto Him, All these things have I kept from my youth up: what lack I yet? Jesus said unto him, If thou wilt be perfect, go and sell that thou hast, and give to the poor, and thou shalt have treasure in heaven: and come and follow Me. But when the young man heard that saying, he went away sorrowful: for he had great possessions* (Matthew 19:16-22).

The young man's problem was not that he was wealthy, but that his wealth was more important to him than following Jesus; more important, even, than obtaining eternal life. When faced with the choice between his wealth—the *true* "god" in his life—and following Jesus, he chose his wealth and "went away sorrowful." His great riches blinded him to what was truly important.

That same blindness afflicts our generation. Many men today live for nothing else than making money and acquiring possessions. Greed breeds selfishness. Those who pursue prosperity as the main focus of their lives are interested only in enriching themselves. They have no room in their hearts for anyone else. Their attitude is, "I worked for mine, they can work for theirs." The sad truth is that no matter how much they have, it is never enough. King Solomon in his wisdom wrote, "He that loveth silver shall not be satisfied with silver; nor he that loveth abundance with increase: this is also vanity" (Eccl. 5:10).

In fact, all man's pursuits are "vanity" if they exclude God. Jesus was very clear about what is really important:

And when He had called the people unto Him with His disciples also, He said unto them, Whosoever will come after Me, let him deny himself, and take up his cross, and follow Me. For whosoever will save his life shall lose it; but whosoever shall lose his life for My sake and the gospel's, the same shall save it. For what shall it profit a man, if he shall gain the whole world, and lose his own soul? Or what shall a man give in exchange for his soul? (Mark 8:34-37)

Men of the world pursue the things of the world and end up, eventually, with *nothing*. God-style men pursue the things of God. Finding the "pearl of great price"—the Kingdom of Heaven—they sell all they have to obtain it (see Mt. 13:45-46). True wealth, prosperity and satisfaction are found nowhere else.

Perversion

Perversion (which is not a popular word these days) is another reason for the shortage of males in their proper roles in our society. Many who have chosen homosexual lifestyles are actively striving to achieve legal rights and protection for their choice, even though that choice violates the plan and law of God for mankind. Gay men took the lead in "coming out of the closet," and it wasn't long before women followed. Now gay and lesbian groups are ever before us, demanding that we accept their lifestyles. It is "politically incorrect" to call it "perversion"; "alternative lifestyle" is now the acceptable term.

Society's changing attitude toward morality and sexual behavior doesn't change the Word of God, which speaks very clearly of *two genders* of mankind: "So God created man in His own image, in the image of God created He him; *male and female* created He them" (Gen. 1:27). God's plan was for male and female, man and woman, to be united together in a completed unity as husband and wife: "Therefore shall a man leave his father and his mother, and shall cleave unto his wife: and they shall be one flesh" (Gen. 2:24). Later, as recorded in Genesis chapter 19, God destroyed the cities of Sodom and Gomorrah for the sin of homosexual perversion.

In other places as well, Scripture leaves no doubt that homosexuality is not simply an "alternative lifestyle"; it is a perversion that is contrary to God's law and design. The apostle Paul wrote to the Corinthians:

> *Do you not know that the unrighteous will not inherit the kingdom of God? Do not be deceived. Neither fornicators, nor idolaters, nor adulterers, nor homosexuals, nor sodomites, nor thieves, nor covetous, nor drunkards, nor revilers, nor extortioners will inherit the kingdom of God* (First Corinthians 6:9-10 NKJ).

Paul also had this to say to the Romans concerning "unrighteous" and "ungodly" men:

> *Therefore God also gave them up to uncleanness, in the lusts of their hearts, to dishonor their bodies among themselves, who exchanged the truth of God for the lie, and worshiped and served the creature rather than the Creator,*

who is blessed forever. Amen. For this reason God gave them up to vile passions. For even their women exchanged the natural use for what is against nature. Likewise also the men, leaving the natural use of the woman, burned in their lust for one another, men with men committing what is shameful, and receiving in themselves the penalty of their error which was due (Romans 1:24-27 NKJ).

Perversion is not only a satanic deception that takes a man away from his proper God-given role, but it is also a sin that destroys his nature and desire to be a man. When men turn to other men for sex and same-sex marriages they are no longer fulfilling the lifestyle and role that God designed for them.

Chapter Three

Despising the Birthright

But if anyone does not provide for his own, and especially for those of his household, he has denied the faith and is worse than an unbeliever (1Timothy 5:8 NKJ).

President Harry Truman had a sign on his desk that said, "The buck stops here." This meant that issues that came to him, whether good or bad, would not be passed off to others or avoided. Truman understood that good leadership meant being willing to face challenges and problems, to risk failure, to make decisions, to act decisively, and to be prepared to live with the consequences of those decisions and actions. In short, he accepted the *responsibility* that came with his office.

It seems that fewer and fewer people today are willing to accept responsibility for their actions, attitudes, or words. Victimization has become a popular theme in recent years. No one is responsible; everyone is a "victim." Our social, emotional, or moral problems are the results of poverty or a negative environment or abuse or discrimination; therefore we cannot be held personally responsible. This mindset affects both genders across a wide spectrum of experience.

Families all across America are suffering and struggling because the adult males—the husbands and fathers—in the home (or who *should be* in the home) have failed or refused to accept their God-given responsibility and position as head of the home. Some of the consequences are staggering: teen pregnancies, abortion, out-of-wedlock births, domestic violence, gang violence, inner-city crime, suburban crime, rape, vagrancy, truancy, drug abuse, alcohol abuse, AIDS, and other sexually-transmitted diseases. Now to be sure, there are many other factors in our society that contribute to these problems, but the absence of responsible, stable, positive male leadership in the home is certainly one of the most significant.

Esau's Birthright

Dysfunctional families are nothing new—the Bible is full of them. Parental favoritism, sibling rivalry and hatred, blended families, adultery, incest, rebellion, deception, treachery; all these and more were realities in many biblical families, even those of the patriarchs and other godly men and women. The family of Isaac is a good example.

Isaac, the son of Abraham, and his wife, Rebekah, had two sons, Jacob and Esau. Genesis chapter 25 records an event between the two brothers that, although seemingly insignificant at the time, had great importance for the future:

> *Now Jacob cooked a stew; and Esau came in from the field, and he was weary. And Esau said to Jacob, "Please feed me with that same red stew, for I am weary." Therefore his name was called Edom. But Jacob said, "Sell me your birthright as of this day." And Esau said, "Look, I am about to die; so what is this birthright to me?" Then Jacob said, "Swear to me as of this day." So he swore to him, and sold his birthright to Jacob. And Jacob gave Esau bread and stew of lentils; then he ate and drank, arose, and went his way. Thus Esau despised his birthright* (Genesis 25:29-34 NKJ).

Despising the Birthright

Jacob and Esau were twins, but because Esau was born first, he stood to succeed Isaac as head of the family and inherit a double share of the estate. As the firstborn, the birthright was his, along with the blessing that went with it. The birthright was a great privilege of *position* in the family, but it carried a great *responsibility* also.

By selling his birthright to his brother for nothing more than a bowl of stew, Esau showed how little regard he had for his position in the family and for the responsibility that was his. In despising his birthright, Esau showed his unwillingness and unworthiness to fill the role of leadership that was his by right as the firstborn. He was more interested in doing his own thing and coming and going as he pleased without being tied down by family leadership responsibilities.

God was not taken by surprise by Esau's character flaws. In fact, when Jacob and Esau were born, the Lord had told their mother, Rebekah, that the elder (Esau) would serve the younger (Jacob) (see Gen. 25:23). God's plan all along was to bless Jacob and fulfill His promises through Jacob's line, but Esau still bore the responsibility and the consequences for his actions. When he sold his birthright, Esau also forfeited all claim or right to the blessing that went with it (see Gen. 27:1-40).

The roots of Esau's failure were character and spiritual deficiencies. He had little regard for the promises that God had made to his grandfather, Abraham, and his father, Isaac. As a matter of fact, Esau had little regard for God. The writer of Hebrews described Esau as a

> *...profane person...who for one morsel of meat sold his birthright. For ye know how that afterward, when he would have inherited the blessing, he was rejected: for he found no place of repentance, though he sought it carefully with tears* (Hebrews 12:16-17).

Profane means godless, someone with no relationship or affinity to God. Esau was worldly-minded with no inclination for or interest in spiritual things. He cut himself off from the promises and blessings of God that could have been his. Esau's descendants, the people known as the Edomites, opposed God's people, Israel, for centuries until they were defeated, absorbed, and disappeared from history.

Like Esau, many men today have "despised their birthright," forsaking their God-given *privilege* and divinely ordained *responsibility* as the leaders of their families. Some of them have grown up never knowing their role in God's plan in the first place. These "Esau-style" men are profane and worldly-minded, giving little or no thought to God in their lives; rather, they selfishly pursue their own pleasure and live for the moment.

The Cost of Irresponsibility

The Bible teaches that one day we will all stand before God to give an accounting of our lives. I believe that we men will be held accountable especially for how we have discharged our responsibility toward our families and loved ones. Consider again Paul's words to Timothy:

> *But if anyone does not provide for his own, and especially for those of his household, he has denied the faith and is worse than an unbeliever* (1 Timothy 5:8 NKJ).

Jesus Himself gave us an example to show us how important this is. While He was hanging on the cross, Jesus committed Mary, His mother, into the care of the apostle John (see Jn. 19:25-27). Mary was apparently a widow at this time, and responsibility for her welfare now lay on Jesus as the firstborn son.

Matthew records a parable of Jesus that illustrates the rewards of meeting one's responsibilities and the consequences of neglecting them:

> *For the kingdom of heaven is as a man travelling into a far country, who called his own servants, and delivered unto them his goods. And unto one he gave five talents, to another two, and to another one; to every man according to his several ability; and straightway took his journey.*

> *Then he that had received the five talents went and traded with the same, and made them other five talents. And likewise he that had received two, he also gained other two. But he that had received one went and digged in the earth, and hid his lord's money* (Matthew 25:14-18).

When the man returned from his journey, he called his servants to account. The first two, who had doubled the amount given them, brought the money before their master. He praised them for their faithfulness and gave them greater responsibility, saying, "Well done, thou good and faithful servant: thou hast been faithful over a few things, I will make thee ruler over many things: enter thou into the joy of thy lord" (Mt. 25:21,23). The third servant received no commendation, for he had done nothing. Instead of bringing the increase and a testimony of faithfulness, he brought excuses and brought down on his head the wrath of his master:

> *...Thou wicked and slothful servant...Thou oughtest therefore to have put my money to the exchangers, and then at my coming I should have received mine own with usury. Take therefore the talent from him, and give it unto him which hath ten talents. For unto every one that hath shall be given, and he shall have abundance: but from him that hath not shall be taken away even that which he hath. And cast ye the unprofitable servant into outer darkness: there shall be weeping and gnashing of teeth* (Matthew 25:26-30).

God takes it seriously when we disobey Him. The cost of irresponsibility is high.

Reclaiming the Birthright

Esau sold his birthright to his brother, Jacob, because he placed no value on it. Apparently he changed his mind later, because when Esau discovered that his father, Isaac, had been tricked by Jacob and Rebekah into giving Jacob the blessing of the firstborn, he complained to his father about both his blessing and his lost birthright:

And he said, Is not he rightly named Jacob? for he hath supplanted me these two times: he took away my birthright; and, behold, now he hath taken away my blessing. And he said, Hast thou not reserved a blessing for me? (Genesis 27:36)

For Esau, there was no way back. His birthright and his blessing were gone forever. No matter how much regret, no matter how much remorse, no matter how many tears, it was too late.

Unlike Esau, it is not too late for us to reclaim our "birthright" as men. God has established in His plan for men to hold the headship in our families. This does not mean being a dictator or exercising absolute control over everything our wives and children do. It does mean leadership as servants of Christ, motivated by love. We have a God-given responsibility to live as godly men in a godless world, as godly husbands to our wives and as godly fathers to our children.

Have you been living as a "man of the world," styling the things of the flesh rather than the things of the Spirit? Have you "despised your birthright," failing to live up to your responsibility as the head of your home? Maybe you are like I was for the first 38 years of my life—without Christ and without a clue as to how to live as a true man. You can begin today to be different, to be a God-style man. The apostle Paul wrote:

That if thou shalt confess with thy mouth the Lord Jesus, and shalt believe in thine heart that God hath raised Him from the dead, thou shalt be saved. For with the heart man believeth unto righteousness; and with the mouth confession is made unto salvation (Romans 10:9-10).

Confess Jesus as Lord today. Let Him save you. Let Him make you into the man He wants you to be, a God-style man.

Maybe you already know Christ, but have still been living like a worldly minded "Esau-style" man. You need to reclaim your

Despising the Birthright

birthright and take up your God-given privilege and responsibility in your home and family. Restoration is possible. John wrote:

If we confess our sins, he is faithful and just to forgive us our sins, and to cleanse us from all unrighteousness (1 John 1:9).

Confess to the Lord that you have been an "Esau-style" man. Claim His forgiveness and let Him restore you to your birthright. You might want to pray as David did when he confessed his sin to God:

Create in me a clean heart, O God; and renew a right spirit within me. Cast me not away from Thy presence; and take not Thy Holy Spirit from me. Restore unto me the joy of Thy salvation; and uphold me with Thy free spirit (Psalm 51:10-12).

Whatever you need to do, it is never too late to start. Do it now.

Part Two

God's Plan for Men

He hath showed thee, O man, what is good; and what doth the Lord require of thee, but to do justly, and to love mercy, and to walk humbly with thy God? (Micah 6:8)

And now, Israel, what doth the Lord thy God require of thee, but to fear the Lord thy God, to walk in all His ways, and to love Him, and to serve the Lord thy God with all thy heart and with all thy soul, to keep the commandments of the Lord, and His statutes, which I command thee this day for thy good? (Deuteronomy 10:12-13)

Chapter Four

Priest

*And ye shall be unto me a **kingdom of priests**, and an holy nation. These are the words which thou shalt speak unto the children of Israel* (Exodus 19:6).

*And from Jesus Christ, who...hath made us kings and **priests unto God** and His Father...* (Revelation 1:5-6).

*But ye are a chosen generation, **a royal priesthood**, an holy nation, a peculiar people; that ye should show forth the praises of Him who hath called you out of darkness into His marvellous light* (1 Peter 2:9).

Well, men, how does it feel to be a priest?

"Now wait a minute, Conway," I can hear you protesting, "just what do you mean by that?" I mean that according to the Bible, we are *all* priests. This includes everyone who is a child of God, each person who names the name of Christ, whether man, woman, boy, or girl. In Exodus 19:6, God told Moses that the Israelites were unto Him a "kingdom of priests." The apostle John refers to the Church as "priests unto God" (see Rev. 1:6), while Peter calls the Body of Christ "a royal priesthood" (see 1 Pet. 2:9).

As priests, we are called of God to proclaim His love and grace—the good news of Jesus Christ—to a lost world or, in Peter's words, to "show forth the praises of Him who hath called [us] out of darkness into His marvellous light" (1 Pet. 2:9b). Although this "royal priesthood" includes both genders, male and female, I believe God has made men priests in a wider dimension as well.

In God's original plan, He has assigned the man—the male—to the position of *headship* in the family. This is a priority of *position*, *not* an indication of any superiority or greater personhood or worth of husbands over wives, or of men over women. The apostle Paul wrote, "For the husband is the head of the wife, even as Christ is the head of the church: and He is the saviour of the body" (Eph. 5:23). This position of headship means that we men are in the role of priests—the primary spiritual leaders—in our families. As such, we are responsible before God for the spiritual environment and direction of our families.

One of the clearest Scripture passages on our priestly function as men in our families is found in the Book of Deuteronomy:

Hear, O Israel: The Lord our God is one Lord: and thou shalt love the Lord thy God with all thine heart, and with all thy soul, and with all thy might. And these words, which I command thee this day, shall be in thine heart: and thou shalt teach them diligently unto thy children, and shalt talk of them when thou sittest in thine house, and when thou walkest by the way, and when thou liest down, and when thou risest up. And thou shalt bind them for a sign upon thine hand, and they shall be as frontlets between thine eyes. And thou shalt write them upon the posts of thy house, and on thy gates (Deuteronomy 6:4-9).

As priests, we are to *love* God, *teach* His ways, *walk* in His ways, and *witness* to His ways.

Love the Lord God Supremely

If we are to be effective as priests in our families, our first priority is to learn to love the Lord our God above all else: "And thou shalt *love the Lord thy God* with all thine *heart*, and with all thy *soul*, and with all thy *might*" (Deut. 6:5). This means that we are to love God with everything we are—with our whole being. Nothing is more important. In Matthew 22:38-39 Jesus called this the "first and great commandment," with the second greatest similar to it: to love our neighbors as ourselves. He then said, "On these two commandments hang all the law and the prophets" (Mt. 22:40).

Everything depends on our love for God. If we do not love God as we should, nothing else in our lives will be in proper order. We won't know how to properly relate to family members or anybody else. Our sense of values, our concept of what is truly important, our moral conscience, and our character all will be distorted. When we are properly related to God, we will also be properly related to other people, and our lives will fall into line. This doesn't mean that we will never have difficulties, but it does mean that we will know who we are and where we are headed. Our love for God will be a spiritual and moral compass that will guide us into becoming the priestly men, the spiritual men, the "God-style" men He wants us to be.

What does it mean to love God? It means to acknowledge Him in all our ways (see Prov. 3:6), showing Him respect and reverence, and obeying His commands. It means trusting Him and surrendering our lives completely to His control. It means seeking daily to know Him more and do His will. Paul summed it up well when he wrote, "For to me to live is Christ, and to die is gain" (Phil. 1:21).

The Bible not only instructs us to love God, but it is full of promises for those who do. Consider these promises, which barely scratch the surface of God's promises to those who love Him:

> ...*I command thee this day to love the Lord thy God, to* **walk** *in His ways, and to* **keep** *His commandments and His*

*statutes and His judgments, **that thou mayest live and multiply:** and the Lord thy **God shall bless thee in the land** whither thou goest to possess it* (Deuteronomy 30:16).

*O love the Lord, all ye His saints: for **the Lord preserveth the faithful**, and plentifully rewardeth the proud doer* (Psalm 31:23).

If ye love Me, keep My commandments....*He that hath My commandments, and keepeth them, he it is that loveth Me: and **he that loveth Me shall be loved of My Father**, and I will love him, and will manifest Myself to him*....*If a man love Me, he will keep My words: and My Father will love him, and **We will come unto him, and make Our abode with him*** (John 14:15,21,23).

*And we know that **all things work together for good to them that love God**, to them who are the called according to His purpose* (Romans 8:28).

*But as it is written, **Eye hath not seen, nor ear heard, neither have entered into the heart of man, the things which God hath prepared for them that love Him*** (1 Corinthians 2:9).

God-style men recognize and acknowledge their role as priests in their families, and seek first of all to love God supremely.

Teach the Lord's Ways Diligently

If our first priority as priests is to love God with all our hearts, our second is to teach God's ways to our children and others under our influence so that they may learn to love Him too. The Lord said to Moses:

Thou shalt teach them [God's commandments] *diligently unto thy children, and shalt talk of them when thou sittest in thine house, and when thou walkest by the way, and when thou liest down, and when thou risest up* (Deuteronomy 6:7).

Priest

To "teach diligently" carries the idea of sharpening, as to hone a knife blade on a whetstone. We are to consistently, continually teach the Lord's ways to our children in all the everyday circumstances of life: at home, out in public, at night, in the morning, at all times. It is to be a lifestyle of teaching both by word and by example.

Before I was a Christian, I had no clue what it meant to be a true husband and father, much less a *priest* to my family. It is only God's grace that held our family together during those years. Once I became a true believer, however, and gained knowledge of God's principles and morals, I immediately wanted to pass it on to the rest of the family. I was not the first born-again member in my family—my oldest daughter and my wife became Christians before I did—but I had a priestly concern and sense of responsibility for their spiritual welfare. I tried to encourage a spiritual atmosphere and environment at home, through passing on spiritual knowledge, leading in prayer times, insisting on prayer when things became chaotic, seeking forgiveness from them for all my mistakes as a husband and father, encouraging them to forgive each other after arguments or fights, and trying to lead them into righteous relationships with God. Today, my entire family confesses Christ. God has blessed us mightily.

The Scriptures provide instruction, encouragement, and promises regarding the spiritual training of our children. Paul wrote to the Ephesians:

And, ye fathers, provoke not your children to wrath: ***but bring them up in the nurture and admonition of the Lord*** (Ephesians 6:4).

The Book of Proverbs says:

Train up a child in the way he should go: and when he is old, he will not depart from it (Proverbs 22:6).

So then, as the priests in our homes, we are to create an environment that is conducive to spiritual teaching, nurturing, and growth both by our wives and our children. Our priestly role as godly men extends beyond those four walls into our churches and communities, but it begins in the home. God-style men are committed to teaching and leading their families to know and follow the Lord.

Walk With the Lord Inwardly

We cannot teach or effectively model anything that is not real to us through our own experience. If we are to fulfill our priestly roles as God-style men in our homes, churches, and communities, we must enter into a close, daily, and continuously growing relationship with Christ. Again, the Lord spoke to Moses in Deuteronomy chapter 6:

*And these words, which I command thee this day, shall be **in thine heart**....And thou shalt bind them for a sign **upon thine hand**, and they shall be as frontlets **between thine eyes*** (Deuteronomy 6:6,8).

These verses picture God's Word as being *in our hearts*, as the center of our being and our emotions, *on our hands* as guiding our actions and overall behavior, and *between our eyes*, as the focus of our minds, our thoughts, and reasoning ability. Total identification with the Word of God such as this describes is possible only as we pursue deep, daily, personal fellowship with the Lord.

The Bible frequently refers to this kind of fellowship with God as a "walk":

*...the Lord appeared to Abram, and said unto him, I am the Almighty God; **walk** before Me, and be thou perfect* (Genesis 17:1).

*Ye shall **walk** in all the ways which the Lord your God hath commanded you, that ye may live, and that it may be well with you, and that ye may prolong your days in the land which ye shall possess* (Deuteronomy 5:33).

Priest

> *Therefore thou shalt keep the commandments of the Lord thy God, to **walk** in His ways, and to fear Him* (Deuteronomy 8:6)
>
> *Teach me Thy way, O Lord; I will **walk** in Thy truth: unite my heart to fear Thy name* (Psalm 86:11).
>
> *As ye have therefore received Christ Jesus the Lord, so **walk** ye in Him: Rooted and built up in Him, and stablished in the faith, as ye have been taught, abounding therein with thanksgiving* (Colossians 2:6-7)
>
> *This I say then, **Walk** in the Spirit, and ye shall not fulfil the lust of the flesh* (Galatians 5:16).
>
> *If we live in the Spirit, let us also **walk** in the Spirit* (Galatians 5:25).

How do we cultivate this deep, inward walk with the Lord? We have quite a few tools at our disposal: Bible study, prayer, regular fellowship with other believers at church, the indwelling presence of the Holy Spirit, worship, attendance at Bible conferences and spiritual retreats, and participation in spiritual growth and discipleship organizations such as Promise Keepers®. As we grow in Christ, others will see more and more the fruit of the Spirit become borne in us: love, joy, peace, longsuffering, gentleness, goodness, faith, meekness and temperance (see Gal. 5:22-23; these are dealt with in greater detail in Chapter Eight).

God-style men aggressively pursue a daily, deep, personal and growing relationship with Christ.

Witness to the Lord Outwardly

An inescapable part of priestly responsibility is the testimony of our lives in Christ to other people, not only at home, but also in the church and community. Referring once more to the priestly passage in Deuteronomy chapter 6, we read:

> *And thou shalt write them* [God's commandments] *upon the posts of thy house, and on thy gates* (Deuteronomy 6:9).

Our lives should be such a clear witness to Christ that it would be as if there were a large sign on the front door of our house proclaiming, "Here lives a godly man." I'm not talking about blowing our own horns. Our *lifestyle* should be such as to leave no doubt in the mind of anyone we meet that we are God's men. As we lead our families in the ways of the Lord, it should be clear to all that we can say with Joshua, "As for me and my house, we will serve the Lord" (Josh. 24:15b).

In Genesis 1:28, God told the first human couple to "be fruitful and multiply." I believe that means more than simply sexual reproduction to populate the earth. God also wanted them to be spiritually fruitful. Adam and Eve succeeded on the first part, but they failed miserably on the second part when they ate of the wrong fruit.

According to God's design, when we cultivate our spiritual lives and bear the fruit of the Spirit that He produces in us—when we live in them and let them live in us—other people, lost people, both male and female, will see Christ in us and desire what we have. God's plan is for us to be a witness for Him in the world.

The apostle Peter had this to say about our witness as believers:

But sanctify the Lord God in your hearts: and be ready always to give an answer to every man that asketh you a reason of the hope that is in you with meekness and fear: Having a good conscience; that, whereas they speak evil of you, as of evildoers, they may be ashamed that falsely accuse your good conversation in Christ (1 Peter 3:15-16).

We should always be ready to share our faith with anyone who asks, being able to explain why we believe and tell what Christ has done for us. This too requires a continual, growing relationship with Jesus. Our witness should always be given in a Christ-like spirit of gentleness and reverence. The combination of our *word* of testimony with our *life* of testimony should never give anyone legitimate cause to criticize us or the name of Jesus.

Priest

Although our verbal testimony to Christ is important, most people would rather *see* a sermon than *hear* one anytime. Whether we like it or not, people are watching us, and they will watch us even more closely when they know that we claim to be men of God. They want to see if our *walk* lives up to our *talk*. If it does, doors will open for ministry of all kinds as God brings people across our paths whom He wants to touch through us. If it doesn't, we will have little hope of making a difference in our communities. Our society already has enough hypocrites.

James understood the value of a visual witness as opposed to a strictly verbal one:

What doth it profit, my brethren, though a man say he hath faith, and have not works? can faith save him? If a brother or sister be naked, and destitute of daily food, and one of you say unto them, Depart in peace, be ye warmed and filled; notwithstanding ye give them not those things which are needful to the body; what doth it profit? Even so faith, if it hath not works, is dead, being alone. Yea, a man may say, Thou hast faith, and I have works: show me thy faith without thy works, and I will show thee my faith by my works (James 2:14-18).

Actions *do* speak louder than words. Our words mean nothing if they are not accompanied by appropriate actions. God-style men recognize that a priestly life is to be *lived out* more than *talked about.*

Chapter Five

Provider

And the Lord God took the man, and put him into the garden of Eden to dress it and to keep it (Genesis 2:15).

I like to describe God's plan for men using the "three p's": *priest*, *provider*, and *protector*. We have already looked at the priestly role. In Chapter Six, we will examine the man's role as protector. For now, let's talk about the man (male) as the provider in God's plan.

It wasn't very long ago when there was little confusion about the idea of the man as the provider, or the "breadwinner," of the family. In recent years, particularly since more and more women have begun entering the workplace and pursuing professional careers, the picture has become less clear. The increase in the number of single mothers who have been forced by circumstances to work to support their families has further complicated the issue.

To be sure, in our modern society today, there seems to be no longer a clear-cut distinction of roles between men and women as "providers" for the family. I am not suggesting for a moment that it is wrong for women to work outside the home or to pursue their own careers. Many women need the personal outlet of a job or career. For many others, it is a financial necessity, even when there is a husband in the home who is working to provide for the family. What I *am* saying is that the blurring of "traditional" male-female roles in this area has added to the confusion many men already feel regarding what constitutes true manhood. Many men today are struggling to find where they fit in.

God's plan from the very beginning assigns to the man a provider role. Genesis 2:15 says that Adam was placed in the garden of Eden "to dress it and to keep it." This was even before Eve appeared on the scene in verses 22 and 23. It was Adam's responsibility to care for and work the garden. This charge appears to have been his alone. God's command to "be fruitful and multiply" applied to *both* Adam and Eve: "And God blessed *them* [male *and* female], and God said unto *them* [male *and* female], Be fruitful, and multiply..." (Gen. 1:28a). I don't want to stretch the point too thin, but it seems that the *primary* responsibility for *keeping* the garden was given to Adam, not Eve. So we see that, even in the beginning, part of the man's role was that of a provider.

Destitutes and Deadbeats

Traditionally, our society has seen the male as the chief provider for the family, and for generations there was intense social pressure put upon men who tended to balk at that responsibility. Our own day has seen a sharp rise in the number of males failing in or fleeing from their responsibility to provide for their wives, children, or any other family members who are in need of support. Many states have begun vigorous campaigns to crack down on "deadbeat dads" who are neglecting or refusing to pay the alimony and child support required by the law.

A lot of males today are afraid of commitment or long-term relationships or fatherhood, or anything that will tie them down. Often a young man begins a relationship with a young woman, and his only goal is to get her into bed. He is sexually attracted to her, says all the right words, and does all the right things to convince her that he loves her. He may even believe it himself after awhile. His girlfriend, on the other hand, believing his claims of love and having fallen in love with him, gives in to his insistent requests for sex. Things seem to go along okay until the day she tells him that she is pregnant with his child. Suddenly, all his talk of love goes right out the window. Unable to bear the thought of the responsibility of fatherhood, of providing for and protecting mother and child, or of giving up his freedom, he abruptly leaves her in the lurch and runs off to ruin another life.

Recent studies have reported an increase in the number of children in our country who are living below the poverty level. Many of these children live in homes with no father or other significant adult male influence. The father may be dead, in prison, a drunk, a druggie, or simply nowhere to be found. The mother may have had to remove herself and her children from an abusive and dangerous domestic environment. Whatever the reason, many of these fatherless families face a desperate daily struggle against destitution.

As Christian men, married or single, we have a responsibility to help, not only when members of our own immediate or extended families are involved, but anytime we can lend a hand to a sister in need. She may not need a husband, but she and her children could always use a "big brother" or a true male friend to be available to listen and give support.

The Bible teaches clearly that God Himself is the champion of the outcast and the helpless, the widow and the orphan—anyone who has no one to plead their cause, speak in their behalf, or stand up for them:

A father of the fatherless, a defender of widows, Is God in His holy habitation (Psalm 68:5 NKJ).

Leave thy fatherless children, I will preserve them alive; and let thy widows trust in Me (Jeremiah 49:11).

Pure religion and undefiled before God and the Father is this, To visit the fatherless and widows in their affliction, and to keep himself unspotted from the world (James 1:27).

As men of God who are "styling" ourselves after God, we should grow to become like Him. His concerns should become our concerns, His heart our heart. Giving of ourselves, our time, our labor, our money, or whatever is necessary to help another in need truly reflects the Spirit of Christ and is a mark of a God-style man. The apostle Paul wrote:

I have showed you all things, how that so labouring ye ought to support the weak, and to remember the words of the Lord Jesus, how He said, It is more blessed to give than to receive (Acts 20:35).

Wake Up, Lazybones!

An ancient proverb says, "Charity begins at home." Although that proverb is not from the Bible, the principle behind it is certainly affirmed in Scripture. As men of God, our greatest responsibility, next to our faithfulness to Christ, is devotion to our families. This is true whether we are married or single. God established the family long before He established either the church or the community. God holds us accountable for how we provide for and care for those who depend on us. The young pastor Timothy received these words from Paul, his spiritual father and mentor:

But if any widow has children or grandchildren, let them first learn to show piety at home and to repay their parents; for this is good and acceptable before God....But if anyone does not provide for his own, and especially for those of his household, he has denied the faith and is worse than an unbeliever (1 Timothy 5:4,8 NKJ).

Those are strong words, but they show how seriously God takes this whole issue. According to Paul one of the key identifying marks of true faith is providing for one's own family. When a man loves God, he will love his family, and when he loves his family, he will work hard to provide for their needs and to protect them. To be sure, there are many devoted husbands and fathers who do not acknowledge God, but love of family finds its highest expression in the heart of the man who loves God.

Provider

The tragedy is that far too many men, even in the Church, have failed to understand or accept the importance of this principle. Whether through laziness, ignorance, immaturity, or indifference, they are failing to be the providers they are supposed to be in their families. The Bible has much to say to males in this situation. Consider these:

Go to the ant, thou sluggard; consider her ways, and be wise: which having no guide, overseer, or ruler, provideth her meat in the summer, and gathereth her food in the harvest. How long wilt thou sleep, O sluggard? When wilt thou arise out of thy sleep? Yet a little sleep, a little slumber, a little folding of the hands to sleep: So shall thy poverty come as one that travelleth, and thy want as an armed man (Proverbs 6:6-11).

Slothfulness casteth into a deep sleep; and an idle soul shall suffer hunger (Proverbs 19:15).

Because of laziness the building decays, and through idleness of hands the house leaks (Ecclesiastes 10:18 NKJ).

The desire of the slothful killeth him; for his hands refuse to labour (Proverbs 21:25).

I went by the field of the slothful, and by the vineyard of the man void of understanding; and, lo, it was all grown over with thorns, and nettles had covered the face thereof, and the stone wall thereof was broken down. Then I saw, and considered it well: I looked upon it, and received instruction. Yet a little sleep, a little slumber, a little folding of the hands to sleep: So shall thy poverty come as one that travelleth; and thy want as an armed man (Proverbs 24:30-34).

On the other hand, the Scriptures also give wise counsel and wonderful promises to those who are faithful and diligent in executing their family responsibilities. Look at these examples:

Be thou diligent to know the state of thy flocks, and look well to thy herds (Proverbs 27:23).

Whatsoever thy hand findeth to do, do it with thy might; for there is no work, nor device, nor knowledge, nor wisdom, in the grave, whither thou goest (Ecclesiastes 9:10).

*The soul of the sluggard desireth, and hath nothing: but **the soul of the diligent shall be made fat*** (Proverbs 13:4).

Love not sleep, lest thou come to poverty; open thine eyes, and thou shalt be satisfied with bread (Proverbs 20:13).

Seest thou a man diligent in his business? He shall stand before kings; he shall not stand before mean men (Proverbs 22:29).

*The steps of a good man are ordered by the Lord, and He delights in his way. Though he fall, he shall not be utterly cast down; for the Lord upholds him with His hand. I have been young, and now am old; Yet **I have not seen the righteous forsaken, nor his descendants begging bread*** (Psalm 37:23-25 NKJ).

More Than Money

Even diligence in providing for the needs of one's family can have its pitfalls. There are many men who work hard day after day earning a living and providing food, clothing, shelter, and other physical needs for their wives and children. Some of them—too many of them—live for their jobs, finding their primary identity in their work rather than in their roles as husband and father. As a result, they provide their families with everything *except* the most important thing of all—*themselves*.

Men, part of being the *provider* in God's plan is to provide *ourselves*, to make ourselves *available* to our wives and children. Working to fulfill their physical needs is important, but it is only part of the picture. It's more than money. It's being there—loving, sharing, modeling God's ways, and helping those we love navigate through the rough water and sharp rocks of life.

God-style men know that being providers means giving themselves as completely to their families as they do to the God they love supremely and as completely as Christ gave Himself for His Church.

Chapter Six

Protector

*So when the woman saw that the tree was good for food, that it was pleasant to the eyes, and a tree desirable to make one wise, she took of its fruit and ate. She also gave to **her husband with her**, and he ate....Then the man said, "The woman whom You gave to be with me, she gave me of the tree, and I ate"* (Genesis 3:6,12 NKJ).

Buck-passing began in the garden of Eden. I'm sure you know the story from the third chapter of Genesis: The serpent tempted Eve by questioning her understanding of God's instructions. Then, by questioning those instructions, he appealed to her pride with the thought of becoming like God. As a result, Eve gave in, ate the forbidden fruit, and gave some to Adam, who also ate. God confronted them with their disobedience, and then the excuses began to fly. Adam tried to blame both Eve *and* God: "The *woman* whom *You* gave...me..." (Gen. 3:12). Eve blamed the serpent: "The serpent deceived me..." (Gen. 3:13).

In the verses leading up to all this, the serpent addresses the woman. Have you ever wondered where Adam was during this time? Was he off tending another part of the garden? Was he lying in a hammock taking a nap? No. *Adam was with her the whole time!* Look at the end of verse 6: "She also gave to her husband *with her*, and he ate." Why didn't he say something? Why didn't he remind Eve again of what God had said and redirect her thinking? Instead, she was deceived and ate the fruit. She then gave some to Adam, who apparently ate it with his eyes wide open to what he was doing!

Adam failed to exercise one of his God-given roles: protector. He should have taken the lead, protecting both Eve and himself from the serpent's seduction by reaffirming what God had said and remaining in obedience to Him. Now Eve was intelligent and completely responsible for her own actions, as was Adam, but the greater responsibility lay with Adam because he was the *head* in God's plan. Adam and Eve were equal partners in God's design, of equal worth, value, and personhood. By *position*, however, Adam was the "first among equals."

Like Adam, we men today are responsible as protectors of the women and children in our families, and also like Adam, we have a generally poor track record with it, particularly over the last couple of generations. The increase in our culture of the incidences of spousal abuse, child abuse, domestic violence, and abandonment by husbands, along with the exploitation of women through pornography, have all but buried the concept of manhood as the protector of womanhood in many quarters. To many, it even seems like an out-dated idea.

Regaining Lost Ground

Men, whether we like it or not, we have lost a lot of the esteem and respect in the eyes of women that we once enjoyed, and to a great extent, it is our own fault. In many areas of our world today women feel they can no longer trust men to be their help in any way. I think you would probably agree with me that we men ultimately are responsible for the way our sisters look at us today. Our cocky attitudes (*"Hey, baby, I'm da man!"*), "macho" behavior, and maturity (or lack of it) leave most women completely unimpressed. Often our approach toward women is that of the hunter and conqueror rather than that of seeking a virtuous woman. Even most *men* who "play around" don't want to marry a *woman* who does. If we want to find virtuous women, we need to be virtuous men. The problem, though, is that I am hearing from many of my sisters that virtuous men are hard to find.

There is little in this world to compare to a good reputation in the eyes of men. Most people respect, even admire, men of honesty, honor, and integrity. The Bible certainly recognizes the value of these qualities:

> *A good name is rather to be chosen than great riches, and loving favour rather than silver and gold* (Proverbs 22:1).

> *A good name is better than precious ointment...* (Ecclesiastes 7:1).

A good name requires vigilance and care to maintain. It doesn't take much to damage one's name, and once damaged, it is hard to restore. The Preacher in Ecclesiastes wrote:

> *Dead flies putrefy the perfumer's ointment, and cause it to give off a foul odor; so does a little folly to one respected for wisdom and honor* (Ecclesiastes 10:1 NKJ).

It is high time that we men take every positive step we can take to win back the trust of the women. Unmarried men can earn the respect of unmarried women by showing them respect, courtesy, and esteem in day-to-day contact. Married men, in addition to showing honor and esteem toward their wives, have the same responsibility toward the opposite sex as single men. Extramarital affairs, spousal abuse, child abuse, failure to pay child support, and not being around when needed have really hurt the image of the married man in the eyes of countless women.

God created male and female and put them together as equal partners one for the other. The Bible says, "Therefore shall a man leave his father and his mother, and shall cleave unto his wife: and *they shall be one flesh*" (Gen. 2:24). When men as a whole come to understand the truth of this unity and equality, I believe we will begin to see a real change in our society. Spousal abuse, rape and other violent crimes, out-of-wedlock pregnancies (and births), abortion, and single-parent households will cease to be the critical major problems they currently are. As males assume their proper roles and become positive role models of true men, there will no longer be any reason for the "battle of the sexes." One reason for this is that both males and females will become more secure in their relationships with each other. Each will see the other as a helpmeet the way God intended originally, and will treat each other accordingly.

The time has come for every man at the age of understanding to turn to God for direction and correction in the areas of his life where he finds himself lacking the qualities of a God-style man. The world desperately needs godly men in every arena: home, church, community, religion, politics, education, and business. We must regain the lost ground and earn back the respect we once enjoyed as men. That respect will come as we live in a manner worthy of it. There is no time to lose. We owe it to our children and to our wives, mothers, sisters, girlfriends, all the women in our lives. We owe it to our neighborhoods and to our nation. We owe it to our world and to our God—and we owe it to ourselves.

Treasures to Be Loved and Guarded

Our treasures are those things that we place the highest value on, those things that are most important to us. These are the things that we take the greatest care to preserve and protect. The world, for the most part, sees treasure in terms of material wealth—money, jewelry, and possessions. A tremendous amount of human energy, effort, time, and resources is consumed in the pursuit and preservation of material wealth.

The Word of God takes a totally different view of treasure. Jesus said:

Lay not up for yourselves treasures upon earth, where moth and rust doth corrupt, and where thieves break through and steal: But lay up for yourselves treasures in heaven, where neither moth nor rust doth corrupt, and where thieves do not break through nor steal: For where your treasure is, there will your heart be also (Matthew 6:19-21).

Now certainly, men, our greatest treasure, the "pearl of great price," is our relationship with Jesus Christ. Beyond that, though, our treasure still does not consist in the *things* that we have acquired or in the *money* we make. It is in the *people* who enrich our lives—parents, wives, brothers and sisters, children, cousins, aunts and uncles, nieces and nephews. They truly are treasures worthy of being loved and guarded. As Christian men, we have the privilege and the responsibility to cherish and protect the human treasures God has given us.

What about it, men? Think about the women in your lives. Who are they to you, *treasures* to be cherished and protected or *trophies* to be displayed as symbols of your "manly conquests"? This is not a trivial question. Our society projects many values and messages that make it difficult for men to view women as something other than objects to be conquered, possessed, and used. We need the solid counsel of Scripture to counter the negative and destructive images and ideas we receive from the world around us.

Listen to what the apostle Peter said:

Husbands, likewise, dwell with them with understanding, **giving honor to the wife**, *as to the weaker vessel, and as being heirs together of the grace of life,* **that your prayers may not be hindered** (First Peter 3:7 NKJ).

The word translated "honor" also means "hold in highest esteem." In other words, our wives are treasures to be highly honored and valued. This verse also implies that failure to so honor our wives will harm our fellowship and walk with Christ.

Paul tells us that the honor we are to show our wives is that of self-sacrificing love:

Husbands, love your wives, just as Christ also loved the church and gave Himself for her, *that He might sanctify and cleanse her with the washing of water by the word, that He might present her to Himself a glorious church, not having spot or wrinkle or any such thing, but that she should be holy and without blemish. So* ***husbands ought to love their own wives as their own bodies; he who loves his wife loves himsel….Nevertheless let each one of you in particular so love his own wife as himself***, *and let the wife see that she respects her husband* (Ephesians 5:25-28,33 NKJ).

As husbands, we are to love our wives as we love ourselves. In marriage, "the two become one flesh" (Eph. 5:31). Our love for our wives is to be as Christ's love for His Church. Christ *gave His life* for the Church, and our love and devotion to our wives should be of the same quality. We are our wives' protectors, even to the point of giving our lives for them.

This same attitude of respect, honor, and self-sacrifice applies to unmarried men as well. It applies to your relationships with your mothers, sisters, and other female family members. Any of you who are involved in a serious relationship with a young woman should treat her with the same regard and respect you would want for your own daughter or your sister to receive from a male friend.

Children are also treasures deserving the highest love and protection. One of the most beautiful biblical descriptions of the value of children is found in Psalm 127:

Lo, children are an heritage of the Lord: and the fruit of the womb is his reward. As arrows are in the hand of a mighty man; so are children of the youth. Happy is the man that hath his quiver full of them: they shall not be ashamed, but they shall speak with the enemies in the gate (Psalm 127:3-5).

Children are a "heritage of the Lord." The word "heritage" could also be translated "inheritance," and is similar in idea to treasure. In ancient Jewish thought, children were considered a sure sign of God's blessing. The children God has entrusted to us are precious treasures to be cherished and protected, both physically and spiritually.

For example, my 16-year-old daughter said to me, "Dad, I'm ready to date." As protector of her virginity, I said, "No, you're not," then went on to explain to her how I myself had taken advantage of young girls who had thought *they* were ready, too. And because many fathers don't protect their daughters well enough, a lot of those girls and young women are ending up in date rape or out-of-wedlock pregnancies. Some of them get abortions, facing the guilt and emotional trauma that so often goes with abortion, while others give birth to their babies, but face the challenge of trying to raise a child while still a child themselves. We need to establish clear, Christ-centered, Bible-based standards for our children to protect and guide them in a world that isn't really interested in their welfare.

We are also protectors in the spiritual arena too. This is closely related to our priestly function as husbands, fathers, or the "man of the house." We should be alert to spiritual dangers that threaten our families and ourselves, and we must regularly lift up our families in prayer, both privately and as part of family worship. If we are being the spiritual influences that we should be, our families will look to us for leadership and guidance. We can't afford to let them down. The potential consequences are too frightening. The family is one of satan's primary targets, and he uses any means at his disposal in this world to attack and destroy.

The sooner we men fully realize the seriousness of the situation in our families and others all across America, and the sooner we renew our commitment to be priest, provider, and protector as God designed, the sooner we will begin to see a great moral and spiritual shift in this country away from the present darkness of confusion to the brilliant light of God's truth.

Part Three

"Styling" God

Therefore be imitators of God as dear children (Ephesians 5:1 NKJ).

Chapter Seven

Jesus, Our Example of Manhood

And Jesus increased in wisdom and stature, and in favour with God and man (Luke 2:52).

I said in Chapter One that everybody styles somebody. We all tend to display the characteristics of the role models we adopt or grow up with in life. Some people have little choice in their role models; their options are limited by economy, geography, or culture. In my own case as a very young man, all my role models were negative. I imitated what I saw in the male adults around me: drinking, smoking, profanity, gambling, chasing women, and bragging to other guys about my escapades.

My older brothers, my uncles and many of the other men in my hometown were hardworking men, but when it came to home life, they didn't really give of themselves. They provided food, shelter, clothing—the basics—but felt little obligation to their families beyond that. Some of the men didn't even provide that much. The few men I knew who were family-oriented were looked down on by the others as hen-pecked. The "macho" image was the thing—gambling, drinking, abusing the wife and children. When I first began drinking alcohol at age 13, many of the men, twice my age and older, bragged about how well I could drink. This was the type of behavior that was encouraged. I wanted to grow up to be like those guys. With no other role models for comparison, I didn't know any better. I didn't know about black men who had finished college or who worked as supervisors, managers, or executives.

Just about the only exception to this was the uncle who took me in and raised me after my parents died. He tried to steer me in the right direction, unsuccessfully encouraged me to go to college, and later, after I had some trouble with the law, was instrumental in getting me accepted into the Navy. Yet this uncle was a bootlegger and ran a gambling house in town, so even from him, I received a lot of mixed messages.

I entered adulthood with no concept of what true manhood was all about. This continued to be the case when I got married. I didn't really know how to treat my wife and children the way they deserved to be treated by a husband and father. I had no solid example on which to base my behavior. It was only at the age of 38, when I accepted Christ as my Savior and Lord, that I finally had a perfect example of manhood to follow and began to understand all that I had lacked in that area through the years.

Countless men today are in the condition I was in for those first 38 years—lost without Christ and devoid of the divine, perfect standard of manhood as an alternative to the confusion of images thrown at them by the world. The world has no standard worthy for us to pattern our lives after. Only Jesus Christ provides the role model we need as men. Paul told the Ephesians, "Therefore be *imitators* of God as dear children" (Eph. 5:1 NKJ). In his letter to the Colossians, Paul referred to Jesus as "the *image* of the invisible God" (Col. 1:15a). If we are to imitate God, we must look to Jesus, God's perfect image. Jesus displayed abundantly in His life the qualities of manhood we have already discussed in

Jesus, Our Example of Manhood

this book: acceptance of responsibility and filling the roles of priest, provider, and protector.

Jesus Accepted Responsibility

During His earthly life, Jesus demonstrated responsible behavior. Part of being responsible is accepting legitimate authority and being subject to that authority. Jesus willingly submitted Himself to the authority of His earthly parents and to His heavenly Father. In his Gospel, Luke records the trip to Jerusalem Jesus made at the age of 12. His parents, Mary and Joseph, thinking Him to be in another part of the caravan, accidentally left Him in the city when they headed for home. When they realized his absence, they returned to the city. After searching for several days, they found Him in the temple. Luke wrote that after this, Jesus "...went down with them, and came to Nazareth, and *was subject unto them*...and Jesus increased in wisdom and stature, and in favour with God and man" (Lk. 2:51-52). The word translated "subject" carries the meaning of submitting oneself to the authority of another. Jesus *chose* to be in subjection to them. Because He was responsible in this way, Jesus grew wise and was well-thought of by all.

Jesus also willingly submitted Himself to the authority of God the Father. A good example of this is found in the fifth chapter of John:

> *Then answered Jesus and said unto them, Verily, verily, I say unto you, The Son can do nothing of Himself, but what He seeth the Father do: for what things soever He doeth, these also doeth the Son likewise....I can of Mine own self do nothing: as I hear, I judge: and My judgment is just; because I seek not Mine own will, but the will of the Father which hath sent Me....But I have greater witness than that of John: for the works which the Father hath given Me to finish, the same works that I do, bear witness of Me, that the Father hath sent Me* (John 5:19,30,36).

These verses make it clear that Jesus did not act on His own authority (although as one with the Father, He *could* have). He submitted Himself to do and act only as the Father willed. Jesus accepted the responsibility that He was given and was committed to accomplishing the mission His Father had given Him, regardless of personal cost. This is seen in His attitude in the garden of Gethsemane the night before His crucifixion as He prayed to His Father, "O My Father, if it be possible, let this cup pass from Me: nevertheless not as I will, but as Thou wilt....O My Father, if this cup may not pass away from Me, except I drink it, Thy will be done" (Mt. 26:39b,42b). Jesus followed the will of His Father, even to the cross. Paul wrote, "[Jesus] humbled Himself, and became obedient unto death, even the death of the cross" (Phil. 2:8b).

God-style men recognize and accept legitimate authority in their lives, and they *always* strive to submit to the will of their heavenly Father.

Jesus as Priest

There are many biblical examples showing Jesus in the priestly role. Those that follow are just a sampling.

You will remember from Chapter Four that a God-style man as priest will love God supremely. This was certainly true of Jesus, and that love gave Him a zeal for God and for the honor of God's name. This love and zeal found powerful expression one day when Jesus was at the temple:

> *And Jesus went into the temple of God, and cast out all them that sold and bought in the temple, and overthrew the tables of the moneychangers, and the seats of them that sold doves, and said unto them, It is written, My house shall be called the house of prayer; but ye have made it a den of thieves* (Matthew 21:12-13).

Jesus confronted the religious leaders of His day with a holy boldness that honored God and angered His enemies. Sometimes being a priest for God is risky.

As a priest, Jesus showed us how to overcome sin and temptation in our lives. The writer of Hebrews says that Jesus was "in all points tempted like as we are, yet without sin" (Heb. 4:15).

Jesus, Our Example of Manhood

Luke records that Jesus, "...being full of the Holy Ghost...was led by the Spirit into the wilderness, being forty days tempted of the devil" (Lk. 4:1-2a). After defeating the devil through fasting, prayer, Scripture, and resolute commitment to God, Jesus "returned in the power of the Spirit into Galilee" (Lk. 4:14a). Jesus' example is a powerful lesson and encouragement to us as we confront sin and temptation in our striving to live as God-style men.

A priest also teaches the ways of God to the people. The Gospels are full of examples of Jesus as a priestly teacher. Probably the greatest example is the Sermon on the Mount in Matthew, where at one point Jesus said:

> ***Ye have heard that it hath been said**, Thou shalt love thy neighbour, and hate thine enemy.* ***But I say unto you**, Love your enemies, bless them that curse you, do good to them that hate you, and pray for them which despitefully use you, and persecute you; that ye may be the children of your Father which is in heaven....Be ye therefore perfect, even as your Father which is in heaven is perfect* (Matthew 5:43-45a,48).

Jesus corrected popular conceptions of behavior that were contrary to God's Word and will, and challenged the people to return to God. As priests in our homes, we as men of God should do the same. We should teach and correct and challenge those under our care to become everything that God wants for them and show them the way to Him by word and by example.

A priestly man prays for those under his care. In chapter 17 of his Gospel, John records Jesus' high-priestly prayer for His followers, surely one of the most beautiful and moving prayers in the Bible:

> *I pray for them: I pray not for the world, but for them which Thou hast given Me; for they are Thine....Holy Father, keep through Thine own name those whom Thou hast given Me, that they may be one, as we are....that they might have My joy fulfilled in themselves....Sanctify them*

> *through Thy truth....Neither pray I for these alone, but for them also which shall believe on Me through their word; that they all may be one... Father, I will that they also, whom Thou hast given Me, be with Me where I am...* (John 17:9,11,13,17,20-21,24).

Jesus also modeled for His disciples (and us) servant leadership. True leadership is possible only when one has first learned to serve and to adopt an attitude of personal humility. In John 13:3-15, Jesus is pictured taking a towel and kneeling down to wash the dusty feet of His disciples—a social task for the lowest of slaves. After correcting Peter's misunderstanding when he tried to stop Jesus from washing his feet, the Lord said:

> *...Know ye what I have done to you? Ye call me Master and Lord: and ye say well; for so I am. If I then, your Lord and Master, have washed your feet; ye also ought to wash one another's feet. For I have given you an example, that ye should do as I have done to you* (John 13:12-15).

God-style men lead their families through selfless service in humble submission to God's headship.

Jesus as Provider

The Gospels also show Jesus in the manly role of a provider. He met physical needs:

> *And He commanded the multitude to sit down on the grass, and took the five loaves, and the two fishes, and looking up to heaven, He blessed, and brake, and gave the loaves to His disciples, and the disciples to the multitude. And they did all eat, and were filled: and they took up of the fragments that remained twelve baskets full. And they that had eaten were about five thousand men, beside women and children* (Matthew 14:19-21).

Jesus satisfied spiritual needs:

> *And Jesus entered and passed through Jericho....And when Jesus came to the place, He looked up, and saw him,*

*and said unto him, Zacchaeus, make haste, and come down; for **today I must abide at thy house**. And he made haste, and came down, and received Him joyfully....And Zacchaeus stood, and said unto the Lord; Behold, Lord, the half of my goods I give to the poor; and if I have taken any thing from any man by false accusation, I restore him fourfold. And Jesus said unto him, **This day is salvation come to this house**, forasmuch as he also is a son of Abraham. For the Son of man is come to seek and to save that which was lost* (Luke 19:1,5-6,8-10)

Jesus also prepared for the future needs of His followers:

And I will pray the Father, and He shall give you another Comforter, that He may abide with you for ever; even the Spirit of truth; whom the world cannot receive, because it seeth Him not, neither knoweth Him: but ye know Him; for He dwelleth with you, and shall be in you. I will not leave you comfortless: I will come to you....But the Comforter, which is the Holy Ghost, whom the Father will send in My name, He shall teach you all things, and bring all things to your remembrance, whatsoever I have said unto you (John 14:16-18,26).

Jesus provided bread and fish for 5,000 hungry people; He sought out a hated tax collector and brought him into the kingdom of God; He promised the Holy Spirit as an indwelling Presence of power and wisdom for His disciples. His example shows how thorough and complete our service as providers should be. As God-style men, we must be rightly concerned with the physical *and* spiritual welfare of our families and all those in our care, both now and in the future.

Jesus as Protector

Jesus also models the ideal of manhood as a *protector* and not a predator. First of all, His approach to life and ministry was absolutely non-violent. Violence never was, never has been, and never will be the way of Jesus. On the night when Jesus was arrested, some of His disciples attempted to defend and protect Him. John tells the story:

> *Then Simon Peter having a sword drew it, and smote the high priest's servant, and cut off his right ear. The servant's name was Malchus. Then said Jesus unto Peter, Put up thy sword into the sheath: the cup which My Father hath given Me, shall I not drink it? Then the band and the captain and officers of the Jews took Jesus, and bound Him* (John 18:10-12).

Jesus sharply rebuked Peter for his actions. Luke, in his parallel account, adds that Jesus then touched Malchus' ear and healed him. Later, before Pilate, before the soldiers who beat and mocked Him, and before the Jewish religious leaders who reviled Him, Jesus refused to return the abuse in kind; He remained silent and even prayed for their forgiveness from the cross. *Such is the nature and character of **true** manhood!*

Our Lord also was never one to take advantage of anyone, particularly the weak, the helpless, or the vulnerable. The Samaritan woman of Sychar who met Jesus at Jacob's well (see Jn. 4:5-29) was probably quite alluring and seductive. After all, she had spent a lifetime (and gone through five husbands) making herself attractive to men. Jesus was alone with her and could undoubtedly have "taken advantage" of her. In fact, at first, the woman may have wanted just that. Instead, Jesus honored her personhood and worth and focused on her spiritual need. He never condemned, but He led her to examine her lifestyle on her own and conclude that she needed God's grace and forgiveness.

On another occasion, Jesus faced down a hostile crowd who had brought before Him a woman caught in the very act of adultery (see Jn. 8:3-11). The crowd was interested in trapping Jesus; they cared nothing for the woman. When they insisted that the woman should be stoned under the law, Jesus replied, "He that is without sin among you, let him first cast a stone at her" (Jn. 8:7b). His simple, piercing response convicted their guilty consciences,

Jesus, Our Example of Manhood

and one by one, the mob dispersed, leaving Jesus and the woman alone. Jesus asked her:

> *Woman, where are those thine accusers? hath no man condemned thee? She said, No man, Lord. And Jesus said unto her, Neither do I condemn thee: go, and sin no more* (John 8:10b-11).

Jesus did not excuse her sin, but neither did He condemn her; *He forgave her*. He respected her dignity and worth as a person and showed His love, the divine love of God, for her.

In every way, in every area of life, Jesus displayed the qualities of true manhood, God-style manhood, and He provides the perfect, indeed, the *only* example upon which we can build successful lives as men.

God-style men strive to be *imitators* of God, looking to Jesus for their inspiration and example, patterning their lives after His life, conforming their ways to His ways and their thoughts to His thoughts.

Chapter Eight

Fruit of the Spirit

But the fruit of the Spirit is love, joy, peace, longsuffering, gentleness, goodness, faith, meekness, temperance: against such there is no law (Galatians 5:22-23).

When we look to Jesus as our example in our desire to become God-style men, it is important to consider not only His *life*, but also His *words*. Our Lord had a lot to say about the lives of both the wicked and the righteous. For instance, He said that a person's character will be revealed by the way he lives and acts:

For a good tree bringeth not forth corrupt fruit; neither doth a corrupt tree bring forth good fruit. For every tree is known by his own fruit. For of thorns men do not gather figs, nor of a bramble bush gather they grapes. A good man out of the good treasure of his heart bringeth forth that which is good; and an evil man out of the evil treasure of his heart bringeth forth that which is evil: for of the abundance of the heart his mouth speaketh (Luke 6:43-45).

Jesus said that each of us will be known by the fruit of our lives. Whatever is inside our hearts—that which characterizes our inner nature, whether good or evil—will show itself in our actions, attitudes, and words. It is possible to hide our true selves from others for awhile, perhaps even for years, but eventually who we really are will come out in some form or fashion because every "tree" produces fruit according to its nature.

What does the fruit of *your* life reveal about *your* character? Are you setting the kind of example you really want? Do others see in you the qualities of manhood that will point them to Jesus as the Savior and Lord of their lives? Or does your life display more the characteristics of the world around you? There is really no middle ground: you will either show the fruit of the Spirit of God or the fruit of the world. What is the fruit of the world? The apostle Paul gives a good description:

Now the works of the flesh are evident, which are: adultery, fornication, uncleanness, lewdness, idolatry, sorcery, hatred, contentions, jealousies, outbursts of wrath, selfish ambitions, dissensions, heresies, envy, murders, drunkenness, revelries, and the like; of which I tell you beforehand, just as I also told you in time past, that those who practice such things will not inherit the kingdom of God (Galatians 5:19-21 NKJ).

People whose lives and natures are characterized by such as these show that they are not part of the Kingdom of God; Christ has not transformed their hearts.

In contrast, Paul then listed the spiritual qualities of godly people, the fruit of the Spirit: love, joy, peace, longsuffering, gentleness, goodness, faith, meekness, and temperance (see Gal. 5:22-23). God-style men will display this fruit in their lives as a growing and developing reality. We do not produce this fruit; the Holy Spirit produces it in us. We are the *trees* who *bear* the fruit.

Since the fruit of the Spirit is so important to our lives as Christian men, it will be helpful to examine each one briefly. Although all nine of these apply in every area of life, it will be convenient to consider them in three groups of three: fruit of the

Fruit of the Spirit

inward life (love, joy, peace), fruit of the *outward* life (longsuffering, gentleness, goodness), and fruit of the upward life (faith, meekness, temperance).

Fruit of the Inward Life

The first three of the fruit of the Spirit in Paul's list, love, joy, and peace, are particular qualities of the inner, personal, and devotional life of a godly man. When we are rightly related to God, when His values and will are first in our lives, we will experience an inner peace, a deep sense of joy, and a love for God (and others) like nothing we have ever known.

Love

I don't think it is accidental that love was listed first because it is the fruit that is the root, the foundation, for all the others. In Greek the word is *agape*, which refers to the highest possible kind of love—the divine love of God for His Son, for mankind (even in all our sinfulness), and, especially, for Christians. Love is the essential nature of God, and so should it be for all of us who claim Him as our Father.

This kind of love is more than an emotion or a response to someone else's attitude toward us. Godly love is a deliberate choice. God *chose* to love us, even in our sin. Christ commanded us to love one another, including those outside the faith and those who are difficult to love. The Holy Spirit will produce in us a love that we could never produce on our own.

The greatest expression of this love was Jesus' death on the cross for our sins. It is a sacrificial love, a self-giving love. As we work out this love in our own lives as God-style men, we must give ourselves completely to God in love and give ourselves completely for our loved ones.

Joy

When we love God and give Him first place in our lives, His joy will fill our hearts. *Joy* is different from *happiness*, even though we tend to use the words interchangeably. Happiness is usually determined by and dependent on outward circumstances:

If things are going well, we're happy; if not, then we're unhappy. Joy, on the other hand, is a quality, a sense of delight and wellbeing that does not depend on outward circumstances because it is rooted in the nature of God. We can be joyful even in the midst of trouble, difficulty, or turmoil.

As godly men, a heart full of joy will make a great difference in the way that we look at the world around us and in our attitudes toward our families and friends. Joy breeds hope, hope produces confidence, and all three are powerful weapons against discouragement, fear, and depression.

Peace

Peace is a serenity of heart and mind, a sense of rest and contentment. It is not the "peace" of the world, but a heavenly calmness that Paul describes in Philippians 4:7 as "the peace of God, which passeth all understanding." Jesus said, "Peace I leave with you, My peace I give unto you: not as the world giveth, give I unto you. Let not your heart be troubled, neither let it be afraid" (Jn. 14:27). God's peace is much more than an absence of conflict. In fact, like joy, godly peace can be present despite conflict or external chaos. It is an antidote to the overdoses of fear, worry, strife, and division that the world tries to force-feed us.

A man who has the peace *of* God is a man who is at peace *with* God, with himself, and with his fellow man. He is a source of strength and stability for his loved ones. King David, the Psalmist, wrote, "The Lord will give strength unto His people; the Lord will bless His people with peace" (Ps. 29:11).

These three—love, joy, and peace—are qualities of the inner life of the godly man. They establish a firm foundation upon which the God-style man builds his life, and they overflow from within him to touch everyone that he meets.

Fruit of the Outward Life

The spiritual fruit of longsuffering, gentleness, and goodness relate to the outward life: our attitude and behavior toward others, whether family, friends, acquaintances, or strangers.

Fruit of the Spirit

Longsuffering

An old proverb says, "Patience is a virtue," but, I am afraid, it is a virtue that is rapidly becoming forgotten in our society. It seems we are getting more and more impatient with people, circumstances, and life itself. The godly fruit of longsuffering is sorely needed in a world increasingly filled with hair-triggers, short fuses, and hotheads.

Longsuffering means patience toward hostile, antagonistic, or irritating people. (Sometimes these people may be in our own families!) It is self-restraint in the face of provocation. In other words, men, *don't retaliate.* Don't return evil for evil, a harsh word for a harsh word, or a blow for a blow. It means you don't "blow your top" or "lose your cool." As always, our example is Jesus, who endured abuse, mockery, reviling, humiliation, and death without ever speaking a word to condemn or raising a hand to retaliate.

Gentleness

Many modern versions of the Bible translate this word as "kindness." It refers to moral excellence in character or demeanor. When we exhibit this fruit in our lives, we will have a kindly disposition toward others, and we will truly desire the very best for them, no matter who they are. This is easy to understand and apply with a person close to us—someone we love dearly or value as a friend. But what about that neighbor who is so hard to get along with or that coworker who got the promotion we thought we deserved? That's where the real test comes. This fruit is the opposite of jealousy and envy. Paul used the same word when he wrote to the Ephesians:

> *And be ye **kind** one to another, tenderhearted, forgiving one another, even as God for Christ's sake hath forgiven you* (Ephesians 4:32).

Goodness

Although gentleness refers to a kindly disposition toward others, the fruit of goodness involves kindly *activity* on behalf of others. This fruit in our lives will motivate us to actively seek opportunities to do good for other people. We will become sensitive to their needs and feel compassion toward them. One expression of this quality is a spirit of generosity.

God-style men will genuinely desire, diligently pray for, and actively seek the good of the people within our spheres of influence. This relates particularly to our family members, but it extends to others as well. Even worldly people love those who love them and extend kindness to their friends and family. Desiring and actively seeking the good of others, even of one's enemies, is an other-worldly quality, a divine quality. True men earnestly desire and seek *everyone's* best.

Fruit of the Upward Life

The fruit of the outward life, longsuffering, gentleness and goodness, are rooted in the inner life fruit of love, joy and peace. All these are made possible by the fruit of the *upward* life: our relationship with God through faith, meekness, and temperance.

Faith

Hebrews 11:6 says that without faith it is impossible to please God. The faith that pleases God is more than simple mental assent to His existence. God-pleasing faith trusts completely and totally in God and His unchanging love. It acknowledges Jesus Christ as the Son of God and the Lamb of God, who was slain before the foundation of the world for the sins of all men. God-pleasing faith begins with firm conviction and belief in God's revealed truth, resulting in personal surrender of one's entire life and welfare to Him, which produces godly conduct inspired by that surrender.

God-style men are not only men of faith, but also of *faithfulness*. They remain true to their convictions and to their God, and they never compromise for the sake of convenience or to avoid difficulty. Their families and associates have confidence in their word and integrity. God-style men are faithful men who can be trusted in all things.

Fruit of the Spirit

Meekness

Many modern versions of the Bible translate this word as "gentleness," which is probably better understood today. Meekness is usually taken to mean weakness. Someone who is "meek" is thought to be a "pushover." The meaning of the biblical word is altogether different. This word was often used to refer to a horse that had been broken. Meekness, in this sense, meant "strength under control." This quality of meekness, or gentleness, is closely linked to humility.

A godly man of faith is a humble man. Any time we come face to face with our sinfulness next to God's holiness, we cannot help but be humbled. Isaiah saw the Lord "high and lifted up," and was moved to cry out, "Woe is me! for I am undone; because I am a man of unclean lips, and I dwell in the midst of a people of unclean lips: for mine eyes have seen the King, the Lord of hosts" (see Is. 6:1,5). Only in a spirit of humility can we approach God. It means being aware of our spiritual need and how totally dependent we are on God for everything, even life itself. The fruit of meekness produces a temper of spirit within us that will accept, without resistance or complaint, God's working in our lives as being for our good and His glory.

Temperance

Most people today think of temperance as referring only to abstaining from drinking alcohol. Perhaps the word "self-control" is easier to understand because more than alcohol is involved. Temperance, or self-control, refers to an attitude, a mindset toward all of life. The world encourages the free, unrestrained indulging of all human appetites and desires: physical, mental, and sexual. The temperate, self-controlled man of God recognizes that all appetites and desires were created by God and, when used properly, are sources of satisfaction and fulfillment. He also realizes that the sinfulness of man makes those appetites and desires subject to great abuse and therefore chooses to bring them under the control of God.

Self-control involves willful subjection of ourselves to God and in all things exercising the control of our will under the power of the Spirit of God.

God-style men realize that the fruit of the Spirit is indispensable to their spiritual diet and seek to be open to God so that the qualities of love, joy, peace, longsuffering, gentleness, goodness, faith, meekness, and temperance will be borne abundantly in their lives.

Chapter Nine

Men of God

Watch ye, stand fast in the faith, quit you like men, be strong (1 Corinthians 16:13).

But you, O man of God...pursue righteousness, godliness, faith, love, patience, gentleness. Fight the good fight of faith, lay hold on eternal life, to which you were also called and have confessed the good confession in the presence of many witnesses (1 Timothy 6:11-12 NKJ).

The time has come for true men, God-style men, to stand up boldly and be counted for the Lord. The psalmist said, "Let the redeemed of the Lord say so" (Ps. 107:2a). Our nation and our world are in deep trouble, mired in moral chaos, and stumbling in spiritual blindness. The only hope is for all the people of God to walk in unwavering commitment and obedience to Christ our Lord. We men in particular must once again rise to take the spiritual lead that we have largely surrendered through sin, ignorance, and neglect. The Lord's indictment of Israel recorded in Ezekiel could be spoken about us in our own day:

And I sought for a man among them, that should make up the hedge, and stand in the gap before Me for the land, that I should not destroy it: but I found none (Ezekiel 22:30).

Even now, there is a wind of revival around the world blowing as God has begun to call His people to repentance, cleansing and restoration. Christ is preparing His Bride, His Church, for His return, making her glorious, without spot or wrinkle, holy and without blemish (see Eph. 5:27). As He has done in the past, God is calling and raising up *men* to take the lead in restoring family and country. Will we listen to Him? Will we respond to His challenge to be the men that He has called us to be, not men of the world, but men of God, men of integrity, holiness, wisdom, prayer, the Word, and the Spirit?

Men of Integrity

First of all, God has called us to be men of integrity, scrupulously honest in all our dealings and absolutely committed to the highest standard of spiritual, moral, and ethical values. We are to be men of our word, with a solid reputation for trustworthiness. Honest, spiritual men of integrity are sorely needed in a society that has grown disillusioned and cynical by repeated corruption, immorality, and dishonesty in much public leadership—in business, politics, and even religion.

The benefits of walking in integrity are many:

It provides us with a firm foundation for living: "Judge me, O Lord; for I have walked in mine integrity: I have trusted also in the Lord; therefore *I shall not slide*" (Ps. 26:1).

It brings us into the very presence of God: "And as for me, Thou upholdest me in mine integrity, and *settest me before Thy face* for ever" (Ps. 41:12).

It gives us a trustworthy standard for personal and public conduct: "*The integrity of the upright shall guide them*: but the perverseness of transgressors shall destroy them" (Prov. 11:3).

It enables us to leave a solid legacy of righteousness to our children: "The righteous man walks in his integrity; *his children are blessed* after him" (Prov. 20:7 NKJ).

It helps us focus our minds on positive and healthy things: "Finally, brethren, whatsoever things are *true*, whatsoever things are *honest*, whatsoever things are *just*, whatsoever things are *pure*, whatsoever things are *lovely*, whatsoever things are of *good report*; if there be any *virtue*, and if there be any *praise*, *think on these things*" (Phil. 4:8).

Men of Holiness

If we as Christian men are to make any difference in our families, churches, and communities, we must be committed to lifestyles of personal holiness. To be holy means to be set apart for the sole use and glory of God. In practical application, this means being pure in heart, body, mind, and spirit and daily seeking to be "conformed to the image" of Christ (see Rom. 8:29). God wants us to be holy. He said in Exodus, "And *ye shall be holy men* unto Me..." (Ex. 22:31). The apostle Peter wrote, "But as He which hath called you is holy, so *be ye holy* in all manner of conversation; because it is written, *Be ye holy; for I am holy*" (1 Pet. 1:15-16).

Paul wrote in Romans 12:2 that we are not to be conformed to this world, but transformed by the renewing of our minds. We need to examine our hearts and minds and lay aside any habit, practice, indulgence, or attitude that conforms to the world, rather than to the Spirit of Christ. What about the pornography magazines, men, or the X-rated videos? What about speech laced with profanity or those dirty jokes shared with your buddies at work? How about the beer and the booze? What are you going to do about that jealousy toward that neighbor with the new sports car or the grudge against the brother at church who offended you?

Lay them aside! Get rid of them! Put off "the old man which grows corrupt according to the deceitful lusts" (Eph. 4:22b NKJ) and "...put on the new man which was created according to God, in true righteousness and holiness" (Eph. 4:24 NKJ). Let all lying, stealing, corrupt words, and "bitterness, wrath, anger, clamor... evil speaking...[and] malice" be put away (Eph. 4:25-31 NKJ). Instead, "...be kind to one another, tenderhearted, forgiving one another..." (Eph. 4:32a NKJ). Take up the mind of Christ and practice holiness through prayer, studying God's Word, and learning to deny the old sinful nature, and listen to the new nature of Christ in you.

Men of Wisdom

There are a lot of smart men running around—well-educated, intelligent, filled with *knowledge*—but truly *wise* men are a much rarer breed. That is because just about anyone with a brain can acquire knowledge, but *wisdom* is a divine gift. It cannot be gotten from books. Wisdom also is related to common sense and one's ability to learn from experience. All of us have probably met someone with a lot of "smarts" but no more common sense than a fence post or a person who keeps making the same mistakes and wonders why nothing ever changes (that's one definition of insanity: doing things the same way and expecting different results).

Wisdom involves discernment; the ability to understand the right thing to do and when and how to do it. That is essentially a spiritual quality, not an intellectual one. The Bible leaves no doubt as to the source of wisdom:

> *The fear of the Lord is the beginning of knowledge: but fools despise wisdom and instruction* (Proverbs 1:7).

> *For the Lord giveth wisdom: out of His mouth cometh knowledge and understanding* (Proverbs 2:6).

> *If any of you lack wisdom, let him ask of God, that giveth to all men liberally, and upbraideth not; and it shall be given him* (James 1:5).

> *But the wisdom that is from above is first pure, then peaceable, gentle, willing to yield, full of mercy and good fruits, without partiality and without hypocrisy. Now the fruit of righteousness is sown in peace by those who make peace* (James 3:17-18 NKJ).

Our family members and loved ones need the trustworthy and reliable counsel of wise men of God to help guide them in the challenges, problems, and decisions of life. God-style men seek God's wisdom so that they may live rightly and help others do so as well. Do we lack wisdom? All of us need to follow James' counsel to "ask of God," and He will give it.

Men of Prayer

Prayer is one of the most important and significant ministries that any Christian has, and this is certainly true for God-style men. We are in a unique and wonderful position to affect the state of affairs in our families, churches, and communities and to help bring about God's purposes in the earth through the power of prayer. It is an amazing thing that a sovereign God who is answerable to no one except Himself nevertheless responds to and is moved to act by the prayers of His people. The Lord Himself told King Solomon of the effectiveness of prayer:

> *If My people, which are called by My name, shall humble themselves, and pray, and seek My face, and turn from their wicked ways; then will I hear from heaven, and will forgive their sin, and will heal their land* (2 Chronicles 7:14).

The kind of prayer that moves God is not the quick, thoughtless, repetitious "Now I lay me down to sleep..." variety, but that which is accompanied by a humble spirit, a repentant heart, and a deep hunger for God. Such praying is the result of conscious, disciplined practice. Prayer is a gift from God, but a lifestyle of prayer must be built deliberately, consistently, and diligently.

Throughout the Scriptures we are encouraged, even commanded to pray. Paul told the Thessalonians to "Pray without ceasing" (1 Thess. 5:17), and wrote to the Philippians:

> *Be anxious for nothing, but in everything by prayer and supplication, with thanksgiving, let your requests be made known to God; and the peace of God, which surpasses all*

understanding, will guard your hearts and minds through Christ Jesus (Philippians 4:6-7 NKJ).

As men of God, we have a responsibility to daily, continually pray *for* and *with* our loved ones, teaching them to pray "in everything"; to pray consistently for our church, its leaders, and its members; to pray for unsaved friends and acquaintances; to pray for God's will to be done on earth as it is in heaven; to pray for our nation and its leaders—the list could go on and on. Men of God are men of prayer.

Men of the Word

The bedrock of our faith is the Word of God, the greatest expression of which is Jesus Christ Himself (see Jn. 1:1). Further, God has provided His written Word, the Bible, as a source of revelation, inspiration and instruction to lead us to salvation through His Son, Jesus Christ, and to establish us firmly in our faith. Consider the words of Paul:

All scripture is given by inspiration of God, and is profitable for doctrine, for reproof, for correction, for instruction in righteousness: that the man of God may be perfect, thoroughly furnished unto all good works (2 Timothy 3:16-17).

As men of God, we need to be men of the Word: We must read it, study it, memorize it, proclaim it, and apply it to our lives daily. We need to be engaged in seeking ways to put forth the Word of God, the message of the gospel, as the answer to the problems of mankind in this world. Paul instructed young Timothy to "Study to show thyself approved unto God, a workman that needeth not to be ashamed, rightly dividing the word of truth" (2 Tim. 2:15).

God's Word is also a source of wisdom, instruction, and illumination: "Thy word is a lamp unto my feet, and a light unto my path" (Ps. 119:105); a guard to help us avoid sin: "Thy word have I hid in mine heart, that I might not sin against Thee" (Ps. 119:11); and a source of inspiration for praise, worship, and service:

> *Let the word of Christ dwell in you richly in all wisdom; teaching and admonishing one another in psalms and hymns and spiritual songs, singing with grace in your hearts to the Lord. And whatsoever ye do in word or deed, do all in the name of the Lord Jesus, giving thanks to God and the Father by Him* (Colossians 3:16-17).

Men of God are men of the Word as much as they are men of prayer. The two go hand-in-hand. Let us not neglect either one.

Men of the Spirit

The indwelling Holy Spirit is the divine source of wisdom, inspiration, and power for us to live effectively and victoriously as men of God. His presence in our lives is a proof and a testimony that we are sons of God and heirs along with Jesus to the riches of glory:

> *For as many as are led by the Spirit of God, these are sons of God. For you did not receive the spirit of bondage again to fear, but you received the Spirit of adoption by whom we cry out, "Abba, Father." The Spirit Himself bears witness with our spirit that we are children of God, and if children, then heirs; heirs of God and joint heirs with Christ, if indeed we suffer with Him, that we may also be glorified together* (Romans 8:14-17 NKJ).

We are children of the King of kings! It's high time that we start acting like it! The Holy Spirit makes it possible for us to enjoy a close, personal relationship with the Lord. God-style men seek to live in a manner worthy of their calling and identity as children of God. Paul stated it this way:

> *I, therefore, the prisoner of the Lord, beseech you to walk worthy of the calling with which you were called, with all lowliness and gentleness, with longsuffering, bearing with one another in love, endeavoring to keep the unity of the Spirit in the bond of peace* (Ephesians 4:1-3 NKJ).

Unlike men of the world, who are caught up in every manner of lust and desire of the flesh, men of God follow the leading of the Holy Spirit to fulfill God's purpose and desire and bear holy fruit in their lives:

> *I say then: Walk in the Spirit, and you shall not fulfill the lust of the flesh. For the flesh lusts against the Spirit, and the Spirit against the flesh; and these are contrary to one another, so that you do not do the things that you wish. But if you are led by the Spirit, you are not under the law* (Galatians 5:16-18 NKJ).

What an awesome privilege, responsibility, and opportunity God has given us as men to make a difference in our world. It is only as we pursue the qualities of God-style manhood, however, that we will be able to fulfill the purpose He has for us. Let us pursue these characteristics in our lives. Let us not just talk about being godly men, or hold it out as a dream, let's do it! Men of God, we have been called to rise up in our homes, in our churches, and in our communities to bring them back to Him!

Part Four

Rise Up, O Men of God

Rise up, O men of God!
Have done with lesser things;
Give heart and mind and soul and strength
To serve the King of kings.

Rise up, O men of God!
His kingdom tarries long;
Bring in the day of brotherhood
And end the night of wrong.

Rise up, O men of God!
The church for you doth wait,
Her strength unequal to her task;
Rise up and make her great!

Lift high the cross of Christ!
Tread where His feet have trod;
As brothers of the Son of man,
Rise up, O men of God!

—William P. Merrill

Chapter Ten

Rise Up in the Home

...as for me and my house, we will serve the Lord (Joshua 24:15).

Joshua knew that the secret to a strong home and family was firm commitment to the Lord. As the nation of Israel was poised on the verge of crossing the Jordan River into the promised land, Joshua challenged the people to make a clear choice between serving God or serving the false gods of the pagan nations around them. He knew there could be no middle of the road. After issuing his call, Joshua then set the example by boldly announcing that he and his family ("house") would serve the Lord.

God has called us as Christian men to be "Joshuas" for our families and communities, boldly holding forth the example of commitment and service to the Lord rather than following the ways and ideals of the world. There is no other dependable foundation on which to build. King Solomon knew this to be true as well, for he wrote, "Except the Lord build the house, they labour in vain that build it: except the Lord keep the city, the watchman waketh but in vain" (Ps. 127:1).

At the end of the Sermon on the Mount, Jesus told a parable that stressed the importance of building on a solid foundation:

> *Therefore whosoever heareth these sayings of Mine, and doeth them, I will liken him unto a wise man, which built his house upon a rock: and the rain descended, and the floods came, and the winds blew, and beat upon that house; and it fell not: for it was founded upon a rock. And every one that heareth these sayings of Mine, and doeth them not, shall be likened unto a foolish man, which built his house upon the sand: and the rain descended, and the floods came, and the winds blew, and beat upon that house; and it fell: and great was the fall of it* (Matthew 7:24-27).

On the outside, the two houses looked the same, and as long as the weather was calm and peaceful, there seemed to be little difference between them. Once a storm blew up, however, the true natures of the houses were revealed. The house built on the rock foundation survived while the one built on the sand was washed away.

In First Corinthians 10:4 Paul describes Christ as a spiritual "Rock" from whom all His people drink just as the Israelites drank water from the rock in the wilderness (see Ex. 17:6). The home built on the "Rock" of Jesus Christ will stand even when the storms and pressures of life beat against it from all sides. A home built on any other foundation has no such protection.

Assault on the Family

Today, the home and family are under attack as never before. Godless, mindless, and satanic messages and values bombard our homes relentlessly through radio, television, movies, books, magazines, and the Internet. Activists across the land are seeking to redefine the family according to their particular agendas, whether gay, lesbian, feminist, or whatever, based on the shifting sand of humanistic philosophy rather than on the solid rock of biblical standards.

Rise Up in the Home

There was a time when the values, ethics, and morals our children were taught at home were reinforced by the institutions and structure of the greater society at large. Tragically, this is no longer the case. Our children now are growing up in a society devoid of any clear value system or even a standard for developing one. It is no wonder that more and more of them are ending up in prison, in mental hospitals, as junkies or alcoholics, or dead from suicide or diseases like AIDS. Many of our children are also ending up as teenage parents burdened with babies they are not prepared for and stuck in unskilled, low-paying jobs with few prospects for a brighter future.

More than ever before the home is the place to counteract the negative influences of society. Since our culture no longer reinforces traditional values and morality, the training we give and the examples we set at home must be done with extreme care and thoroughness. Our roles as God-style men are to teach and model the ways of the Lord (*priest*), shield our families, particularly our children, from the negative and destructive influences of the world (*protector*), and to equip them to make their own way as confident, committed men and women of God (*provider*).

Personal Spirituality

It's impossible for us to take people somewhere that we have never been. We will not be able to lead our loved ones to a higher spiritual plane than we are on ourselves. For that reason, fulfilling our calling as God-style men will require the highest possible standard of personal spiritual devotion and holiness at home.

How much time do you spend in prayer each day? How often do you lift up your wife in prayer to the Lord? Your children? Your brothers and sisters? Your parents? Your cousins, nieces and nephews? Do you have a regular schedule for prayer, or do you grab it as you can? I cannot overestimate the value of consistent, regular prayer. Take a careful look at your personal schedule. Considering your job and other obligations and commitments, when would you have the most time to devote to prayer on a regular basis? Would early morning work best? What about your lunch hour or at night before bed? If you do not have a regular habit of prayer, let me challenge you to establish one now. You may find it necessary to adjust your life a little bit for it to work, but it would be hard to find a better and more profitable use of your time.

Another important area of personal spirituality to exercise is regular Bible study. When we approach God's Word with the desire and expectancy to learn from it, the Holy Spirit will open its treasures to our understanding. The Bible contains truths and principles that provide sure and reliable counsel for us as we meet the challenges of daily living. The writer of Hebrews said, "For the word of God is living and powerful, and sharper than any two-edged sword, piercing even to the division of soul and spirit, and of joints and marrow, and is a discerner of the thoughts and intents of the heart" (Heb. 4:12 NKJ) Such a *living* word of a *living* God applies to us today as much as it did to the earliest believers, and can change our lives and those of our families if we will let it. God's Word is always new and fresh, never stale or out of fashion. Our loved ones look to us for spiritual leadership, and we can guide them and help them grow in Christ only when we ourselves have a continually fresh and growing relationship with Him.

Our families (as well as other people) are watching us to see if our actions back up our words, so, men, let's be careful about our walk—the example we set by our personal conduct. It's easy to slip into inconsistent or dishonest modes of behavior about the "little things" that we don't think of as very important: a little lie or deception here, an impatient or ill-considered word there, or merely general inattention to the finer points of ethics and honesty. Little compromises build up over time to become major character flaws. There's already enough hypocrisy in the world; let's allow no place for it in our lives. Paul pointed out the importance of this when he wrote, "Abstain from all appearance of evil" (1 Thess. 5:22). That means in *everything*, even the little things.

The Wife of Your Youth

Men, we live in a culture today where marital infidelity does not carry the same sense of public moral outrage and scandal that it once did. To be sure, it has always been with us, but it is only in our century that it has "come out of the closet," so to speak, so that public knowledge of a man's "cheating" has little effect on his reputation or standing in society. In fact, it seems that such behavior is almost expected now, or at least taken for granted, particularly among leaders of national standing. The general mood among many in our land is, "As long as I am doing okay, and as long as the economy is strong, what our leaders do in their personal lives doesn't matter." It boils down to the question of character. The truth is, character *does* matter. It always has.

One of our problems is that many husbands have bought into the myth that "the grass is greener in another man's field," and they have lost sight of the treasure that is right by their sides. For some men who have the "hunter-conqueror" mentality, the "conquered"—the wife safely at home—loses her appeal to him, and off he goes after another "conquest." Other men, oblivious to their own inadequacies, seek fulfillment in the arms of another woman.

Husbands, we each need to open our eyes and cherish and treasure the wives God has blessed us with. Listen to what some of the wisdom books of the Bible have to say about our wives:

> *Let your fountain be blessed, and **rejoice with the wife of your youth**. As a loving deer and a graceful doe, let her breasts satisfy you at all times; and always be enraptured with her love* (Proverbs 5:18-19 NKJ).

> ***He who finds a wife finds a good thing**, and obtains favor from the Lord* (Proverbs 18:22 NKJ).

> ***Live joyfully with the wife whom you love** all the days of your vain life which He has given you under the sun, all your days of vanity; for that is your portion in life, and in*

the labor which you perform under the sun (Ecclesiastes 9:9 NKJ).

Who can find a virtuous wife? For her worth is far above rubies*. The heart of her husband safely trusts her; so he will have no lack of gain. She does him good and not evil all the days of her life* (Proverbs 31:10-12 NKJ).

Our wives need and deserve all the love, respect, esteem, honor, and affirmation that we can give them. They need us to be attentive to them, to be sensitive and responsive to their needs. Maybe we need to put down the newspaper or turn off the television and *listen* to them. One of the most common problems in marriages today is poor communication. Husbands and wives talk less and less, and the emotional distance between them increases until one or the other, or both, begin seeking satisfaction elsewhere. Divorce is a common result. Let's *talk* with our wives. And it should not be just surface chit-chat, but we must really talk with them about hopes, dreams, goals, fears, joys, sorrows—all the things that make up life.

Another thing we husbands need to do is *be available* to our wives. Many husbands have turned responsibility at home over to their wives, particularly where spiritual leadership is concerned. Often, their attitude is, "I've worked all day, now I'm just going to relax. Keeping the home is *her* job." By God's design, husbands are the *head* of the home. We need to take up our proper role of leadership; not dictatorship, but partners together with our wives in building a home where Christ is honored and where all family members grow strong physically, mentally, emotionally, and spiritually.

The Children of Your Inheritance

Fathers, our children look to us for an example to follow, for guidance in life, and for an *approachable* love. We need to be available to them, accessible when they need to talk or to cry or simply to be held close. Our children need to see a father who honors, loves, and respects their mother. Don't be afraid to openly

Rise Up in the Home

show affection for your wife in front of your children. It helps your children feel secure and safe when they know that mom and dad love each other and have a strong relationship. Don't be afraid to openly show affection for your children, either. They need to *see* love in action to understand that love is more than just a word or an emotion, that it is something lived out every day.

Our children need to see us as a good example in our attitudes, our work ethic, and our speech. They need to have a clear understanding of what is acceptable and unacceptable behavior at home and in public. For this reason, we should establish, along with our wives, clear guidelines for our children regarding behavior, standards, and expectations for home life, for dating, for school work, for leisure activities, and for church involvement.

In short, we need to *be involved* in our children's lives on a daily basis, affirming and challenging them to become all they can be personally, professionally and in the Lord, and being there to pick them up when they fall and encourage them to keep going.

As far as the unmarried men are concerned, even though you may not have wives or children of your own, the basic principles here still apply. Consider the women in your life: mother, sisters, nieces, cousins, or that special person you are building a relationship with. All of them need and deserve the same honor, esteem, and respect that are due a wife from her husband. Your younger relatives of both sexes need to see in you a man who respects himself, loves the Lord, and shows Christlike love to them and to everyone else.

When we boldly and in obedience to God take the spiritual lead in our families; when we love our wives as ourselves and in the same way as Christ loves the Church; when we encourage and affirm our children and model the life of Christ before them, we will begin to see our families growing strong in the Spirit and confident in life, and the more families that grow in this way, the greater the change we will see in our society and culture.

Chapter Eleven

Rise Up in the Church

For as we have many members in one body, but all the members do not have the same function, so we, being many, are one body in Christ, and individually members of one another (Romans 12:4-5 NKJ).

Can you remember a time when you had a physical illness or injury where a part of your body was in great pain or did not function correctly? Maybe it was a broken arm or leg, a viral or bacterial infection, or some other condition that required medication or perhaps surgery to correct. Did you notice how the problem in that one part or area of your body affected all the rest of your body? Whenever any part of the body is sick or not doing its job, the entire body suffers.

This is a picture of what happens in the Church, too. In fact, in the New Testament, the Church often is referred to as "the Body of Christ." This is particularly true with the apostle Paul, because it was his favorite expression for the Church. Consider what he wrote to the Corinthians:

For as the body is one and has many members, but all the members of that one body, being many, are one body, so also is Christ. For by one Spirit we were all baptized into one body; whether Jews or Greeks, whether slaves or free; and have all been made to drink into one Spirit. For in fact the body is not one member but many. If the foot should say, "Because I am not a hand, I am not of the body," is it therefore not of the body? And if the ear should say, "Because I am not an eye, I am not of the body," is it therefore not of the body? If the whole body were an eye, where would be the hearing? If the whole were hearing, where would be the smelling? But now God has set the members, each one of them, in the body just as He pleased....that there should be no schism in the body, but that the members should have the same care for one another. And if one member suffers, all the members suffer with it; or if one member is honored, all the members rejoice with it. Now you are the body of Christ, and members individually (1 Corinthians 12:12-18,25-27 NKJ).

Paul is saying here that there is one Body in Christ, His Church, but that Body is made up of many diverse members, individual believers of varying gifts, talents, abilities and functions. Each one is important to the proper functioning of the Body. The Church is one Body in diversity.

One Body in Diversity

As believers in Christ we all have much in common, no matter what our backgrounds may be. We may be male or female, black, white, Hispanic, Asian, or whatever. We may be rich, poor, or in between. We may be young or old, strong or weak. Whoever we are, wherever we come from, we are joined together in a common bond in Jesus Christ. Paul says that "…by one Spirit we were all baptized into one body…and have all been made to drink into one Spirit" (1 Cor. 12:13 NKJ). That common bond removes the barriers of gender, race, nationality, socio-economic status, and any other dividers that human sin and worldliness have erected. The Holy Spirit reveals to us how alike we really are and how

Rise Up in the Church

unimportant are the things we allow to divide us. We all are saved by faith in Christ through repentance of our sin, and we all are born into the Kingdom of God with equal status as joint-heirs with Christ.

At the same time, we each retain our distinct individuality and personhood. The Holy Spirit does not stamp us into cookie-cutter cutouts identical to each other. Our various backgrounds of race, culture, education, genetic endowment, talents, and gifts provide a rich diversity of resources the Lord can and wants to use in each of our churches for His purpose and glory. Each believer is important in this process. We must not evaluate or judge as the world does, which looks at the surface, but as God does, who looks at the heart. In Paul's analogy, the foot, the eye, and the ear are all of equal importance to the body, for they each have a specific function that only they can perform. If any member is failing to function, then the entire body suffers. If any believer is not fulfilling his or her function in the Church, the whole Church is not as effective as it could be.

Much of the modern Church in America has been crippled because so many members are not functioning in their roles in the Body as the Lord intended. Although this involves both genders, what is particularly tragic is how so many men are failing in this area. The sad truth is that in many cases, particular local churches would be forced to fold up and close their doors if it weren't for the faithful women carrying the brunt of the burden of ministry there. Where are the men?

I have no problem at all with women involved in ministry in the church. God's Word makes it clear that *all* believers are called as ministers; *all* believers have ministry functions and responsibilities in the church. The problem is that often women have to carry out their functions, while at the same time carry many of those functions that God intended to be performed by the men. I believe women have legitimate leadership roles in the church, even in the pulpit, but I also believe that God has placed the man in the *position* of headship in the church, with the primary responsibility for leadership. When the Church is functioning properly, I think we will see men and women working *together*, alongside one another in an equal partnership of giftedness and ministry, under the *positional* headship of the men.

This doesn't necessarily mean that the men in the church should dictate to the women what their ministries and functions can and cannot be; rather, they must be sensitive to the purpose and work of the Holy Spirit. For example, I believe that my wife has a ministry in the Church, and I want to give her as much room as she needs to minister according to the gifts and the calling God has given her. At the same time, I need to be faithful in my proper role as pastor and my position of headship. When everyone, man or woman, understands each other's roles, appreciates each other's giftings and callings, and functions in those giftings and callings, the result will be a harmonious Church vibrantly alive and effective in reaching people for Christ.

One Body in Unity

The Church will truly be the Church when the men rise up to assume their leadership positions as God has intended, with all members of the Body functioning in unity of spirit and purpose. This kind of unity is possible only through the presence and power of the Holy Spirit. Look at what Paul wrote to the church at Ephesus. Notice how often the word *one* appears:

> *I, therefore, the prisoner of the Lord, beseech you to walk worthy of the calling with which you were called, with all lowliness and gentleness, with longsuffering, bearing with one another in love, endeavoring to keep the unity of the Spirit in the bond of peace. There is **one** body and **one** Spirit, just as you were called in **one** hope of your calling; **one** Lord, **one** faith, **one** baptism; **one** God and Father of all, who is above all, and through all, and in you all. But to each one of us grace was given according to the measure of Christ's gift....till we all come to the unity of the faith and of the knowledge of the Son of God, to a perfect*

man, to the measure of the stature of the fullness of Christ (Ephesians 4:1-7,13 NKJ).

This passage contains a lot of reminders of principles we have looked at in earlier chapters. Paul tells us to "walk worthy" of our calling as Christians. The characteristics of that walk—lowliness, gentleness, longsuffering, forbearance—are similar to the fruit of the Spirit from Galatians 5:22-23 that we considered in Chapter Eight. The Church that displays these qualities will be a Church that enjoys the "unity of the Spirit in the bond of peace."

Unity means walking together, working together with a common goal and a common spirit, and being inspired by a common vision. Success depends upon the diversity of members exercising their gifts and filling their roles in harmony, so that all services, positions, responsibilities, and ministries are covered. Such oneness is truly a blessing from God and an evidence of spiritual life in the Body. Listen to the psalmist:

> *Behold, how good and how pleasant it is for brethren to dwell together in unity! It is like the precious ointment upon the head, that ran down upon the beard, even Aaron's beard: that went down to the skirts of his garments; as the dew of Hermon, and as the dew that descended upon the mountains of Zion: for there the Lord commanded the blessing, even life for evermore* (Psalm 133:1-3).

Unity is compared to the anointing oil, representing the blessing and favor of God, that sanctified the priests, setting them apart for God's service. It is compared also to the dew of the holy mountain where God spoke the covenant of eternal life to His people. Unity truly is a taste of Heaven!

One Body, Fruitful and Multiplying

When we Christian men in the Church are being the men we are supposed to be, the women in the Church will be free to be the women they are supposed to be, and the Church will become what it is supposed to be: a dynamic, living body, fruitful and multiplying. A living Church is a growing Church, and a growing Church is a reproducing Church. Since the Church is the people, not the building, a reproducing church reaches other people one by one, person-to-person. That is the biblical pattern for carrying the good news of Jesus Christ to the world. It is the pattern that Jesus used. It is the pattern that we too must use if we hope to win our cities and towns, our states, and our nation—if we dream of taking the streets and the ghettos and the neighborhoods for Jesus or of reaching the gangs with the gospel. The Church needs to reach out to the lost, particularly to the millions of men who, caught up in the values and philosophies of this world, have no concept of the love of God or of the nature of true manhood as modeled by Jesus Christ.

It is time for Christian men everywhere to rise up in the Church, take the lead, and set the example. William P. Merrill, a pastor and hymn writer, wrote:

> "Rise up, O men of God!
> The church for you doth wait,
> Her strength unequal to her task;
> Rise up, and make her great!"

That is our challenge, our call, our privilege, and to accomplish it, we must work together. No one can do it alone. The pastor certainly can't, although some have tried, and many more have been forced to carry too heavy a burden because of insufficient support and help from the people. That's one reason so many pastors have heart attacks, strokes, and other health problems. Some even die prematurely. As pictured in the twenty-third Psalm, the pastor, just like the Great Shepherd, is the shepherd of his flock. He is charged with the responsibility for feeding and nurturing the sheep, helping them understand and be prepared for the dangers they face from the wolves and lions in the world ready to destroy them, and making sure that they are spiritually healthy. The pastor also has the responsibility to help train the people under his care to become shepherds themselves, bringing

Rise Up in the Church

other lost sheep into the fold. Pastors need help, though. They can no more go it alone than Moses could, who delegated authority to trustworthy men to help him care for the Israelites, or than Jesus could, who chose 12 men to train and prepare to work with Him.

Rise up, men of God! The Church needs godly men to minister alongside the pastor as deacons and elders, helping to care for the flock, visit and pray for the sick, feed the hungry, witness to the lost, and stand up for Jesus in a culture that desperately needs Him.

Rise up, men of God! Our young people, tomorrow's men and women, the Church and society leaders of the next generation, need to see godliness in action. They need to see holiness and God-love modeled by men who have learned what true manhood is and who live it out consistently every day—manhood God-style.

Rise up, men of God! The Church needs men with teachable spirits, wise and full of the knowledge of the Word of God to be teachers, "rightly dividing the word of truth" for the people (see 2 Tim. 2:15), that they may grow in wisdom and in the knowledge of the Lord.

Rise up, men of God! The Church waits for Spirit-filled men who will exercise their gifts in humility and sincerity and minister in the name and power of Jesus.

Rise up, men of God! The Church and the world wait for you to witness to the saving grace of Jesus Christ.

Rise up, O men of God! Be fruitful and multiply! Rise up in the Church and make her great!

Chapter Twelve

Rise Up in the Community

And I sought for a man among them, that should make up the hedge, and stand in the gap before Me for the land... (Ezekiel 22:30).

And He said to them all, If any man will come after Me, let him deny himself, and take up his cross daily, and follow Me (Luke 9:23).

Changing the world begins at home. When our homes and families are in order, our churches will be in order, and when our homes and churches are in order, our communities will be transformed. When we are the men we are supposed to be at home—husbands, fathers, brothers, sons—our women and children will be free to become all they can be in Christ. When we take up our appropriate responsibilities and leadership in our churches, our churches will become more effective at reaching the lost for Christ and at being a prophetic voice in the land. We will really begin to make a significant difference in our society.

This progression from our closest circles outward is the biblical pattern. Jesus told His disciples:

But ye shall receive power, after that the Holy Ghost is come upon you: and ye shall be witnesses unto Me both in

Jerusalem, and in all Judaea, and in Samaria, and unto the uttermost part of the earth (Acts 1:8).

We are to be witnesses first at home (Jerusalem), then in our communities (Judaea), in the midst of our enemies (Samaria), and finally to the world at large. Our Lord has given us a biblical mandate to be actively involved in changing the moral, spiritual, and social climates in which we live every day. Jesus went where the people were and taught His disciples to do the same thing. While the religious leaders and experts in the Law were busy following their rituals, studying the Law, and avoiding "unclean" people, Jesus was feeding the hungry, healing the sick, and raising the dead.

Jesus is our example and our model for ministry and for engaging society. We cannot change our communities if we avoid contact and involvement with them. As God-style men, our challenge is to be "*in* the world but not *of* the world." We must actively engage our communities for Christ while avoiding contamination by the values and ideals of the world. There are at least four significant ways we can be involved: intercession, sacrificial personal involvement, mentoring, and pursuing restoration and reconciliation between people.

Stand in the Gap

The Lord told the prophet Ezekiel that He looked for a man among the people who would "stand in the gap before Me for the land" to intercede for the nation (see Ezek. 22:30). Today, God still seeks those who will "stand in the gap" and pray for the people. In this day, there is a particularly strong and renewed call for men to take up this ministry.

In October 1997, over 1,000,000 men from all across America gathered at the Mall in Washington, D.C. for "Stand in the Gap," a day of praise, worship, prayer, confession, and repentance. Sponsored by Promise Keepers®, the event was an indicator of a new mood sweeping the land—a renewed hunger for God on the part of men and a desire to serve and honor Him. It is an encouraging sign, but there is still so much to do, so many people to reach.

One of the most important things we can do for our communities as men of God is to commit ourselves to regular, consistent intercessory prayer for them. James said, "The effectual fervent prayer of a righteous man availeth much" (Jas. 5:16b). The leaders, the agencies, the institutions, the schools, the hospitals, the neighborhoods, the churches, the homeless, the poor, the police, the firefighters, the gangs, the drugs; these and countless others are community needs for which we can intercede. The greatest need, of course, is for Jesus Christ and for a general return to the principles, values, and beliefs taught in the Scriptures.

As God-style men, we need to be faithful in intercessory prayer for our cities, towns and neighborhoods, praying as Jesus taught, "Thy kingdom come. Thy will be done in earth, as it is in heaven" (Mt. 6:10).

Take Up Your Cross

Active engagement in intercessory prayer for our communities leads quite naturally to active personal involvement. The longer we pray for needs, the greater our burden will become, along with a growing sense of personal responsibility to get involved. God-style men are called to be more than just believers; we are called to be *disciples*. Discipleship is ministry in action—Christianity with feet and hands. The call to discipleship is a call to risky living and personal sacrifice. Jesus didn't mince any words:

> *...If any man will come after Me, let him deny himself, and take up his cross daily, and follow Me* (Luke 9:23).

To the Roman government, the cross was a device of torture and execution. To Jesus, it was an instrument of personal sacrifice. Jesus gave His very life for us. The call to discipleship is the same. We are called to give our lives in the name of Jesus, not necessarily in physical death (although that too could be required of us), but certainly in service and in the attitude of our hearts.

The apostle Paul certainly understood this self-sacrificing aspect of discipleship, as he encouraged the Romans to present their bodies as a living sacrifice, "holy, acceptable unto God, which is your reasonable service" (Rom. 12:1). Paul knew what he was talking about because he lived it himself. He told the Galatians, "I am crucified with Christ: nevertheless I live; yet not I, but Christ liveth in me: and the life which I now live in the flesh I live by the faith of the Son of God, who loved me, and gave himself for me" (Gal. 2:20). Jesus told us to take up our crosses *daily* and follow Him. A cross is not a pleasant thing to bear. Sometimes it hurts. Sometimes it is dangerous. Sometimes it carries a lot of risk.

Whenever we see something wrong in our community or a problem in a relationship, we have a responsibility to do what we can to help. This doesn't mean being a busybody, butting in where we have no business, but it does mean making ourselves available to those who need help. It means taking a *risk* in order to minister in Jesus' name. Our offer of help may not be accepted; it may even be resented and rejected, but that is part of the risk. We need to be careful too because of today's lawsuit-happy generation. Getting involved carries risks, but just as our Lord sacrificed Himself for us, so we too are called sometimes to sacrifice ourselves for others.

The more the attributes of the Christ-life, the fruit of the Spirit, become real in our daily living and our Christian walk, the more respect we will have in the community, and the more they will begin to seek us out for help and counsel. Our reputations precede us.

I live in a small town in Missouri, and have on numerous occasions gone to the courts, met with parents, and put myself on the line in other ways to help defend and protect and minister to the young people in the city. I have found that as I carry myself as a Christian and a pastor throughout this community, I am held in high regard and respect. That is no brag on me but on the Lord and how He has changed me from the man I once was. As my reputation has grown, I have received invitations to community events—chamber of commerce meetings, baccalaureate services, etc.—to deliver invocations and messages. Sometimes there is risk involved, but what wonderful opportunities they are to rise up and be counted for Christ!

Sometimes I, along with other Christian men and women, have been called in to the local schools to counsel students after a crisis, such as a shooting or the untimely death of a student. Recently, during the final few weeks of the school year, three of us worked diligently with some at-risk children. We met with them at school, during class time, every Friday afternoon. In talking with these young men, I applied an awful lot of Christian principles. I consider it a miracle and a blessing from God that the school system in my town recognizes the importance of ministry and includes it in the schools. That doesn't happen in very many places anymore.

The point I am making is that as Christian men we need to involve ourselves in our communities at every level, taking up our crosses and living the gospel of Jesus Christ wherever we go, whatever we do: on the job, on the street corners, in the grocery store, at Little League games, wherever. The verbal witness of our testimony is important, but the visual witness of our conduct day in and day out makes more of an impact.

Empty Heads

An advertising slogan of a few years ago declared, "A mind is a terrible thing to waste." There are thousands of young men on the streets of our cities and towns whose minds are being wasted through lack of an education, through drugs, through gang violence, through lack of any sense of purpose or meaning for life. As Christian men, we have a call and an opportunity to help turn the tide in the lives of this lost generation of males. One way we can do this is through mentoring.

A mentor is a counselor or guide, someone who tutors another through word and example. It can take many forms. Any type of community activity or organization that provides direct contact with young people can be an opportunity for mentoring—the scouting program, Big Brother, Little League, YMCA, the soup kitchen, the homeless shelter—the list is practically endless.

Somewhere around you there is someone who needs the encouragement, the love, the compassion, the attention, and the wise guidance that you can give. Look around in your community. See what opportunities are available. Consider your own interests and abilities, and decide where you can plug in and get involved. It doesn't even have to be a formal thing. What about the kid down the street who doesn't have a father and could use a good male friend, someone to be like a father to him? What about the kids at church who need someone to do things with them and take them places? The possibilities are limited only by the breadth of your vision and the depth of your imagination.

Many of these "lost" males on the streets, particularly in the black communities, tend to see only two real possibilities to escape: professional sports and entertainment. For the vast majority of these males, neither of these are truly viable options. There are at most only about 5,000 professional athletes in the United States in all sports combined. Against a population of 250,000,000, the odds of becoming a professional athlete are very small. The entertainment field is also very competitive and potentially very destructive. Many "successful" entertainers have disastrous personal lives. It is really difficult to leave any kind of a lasting legacy.

Education is a much better route to go. As mentors, we can give these young men better options and choices, open their eyes to a greater range of possibilities. We can mentor them into the place where they can learn to make better choices and wiser decisions and encourage them to shoot for the stars. Getting a proper education is the starting place.

The Three "R's"

If there are three words that define what is needed for the men in our day and age, then they are *restoration*, *reconciliation*, and

Rise Up in the Community

respect. Men need to be restored to their rightful places in the home, church, and community; they need to be reconciled to God, to themselves, to their families, and to other people, regardless of race or background; and they need to learn to respect themselves and others as persons created in God's image, as well as earn the respect of their families and communities.

As God-style men, we have a calling to restore lost or wandering ones: "Brethren, if a man be overtaken in a fault, ye which are spiritual, restore such an one in the spirit of meekness; considering thyself, lest thou also be tempted" (Gal. 6:1). We are to seek out those who need to be restored, not wait for them to come to us. God has given us a ministry of reconciliation:

And all things are of God, who hath reconciled us to Himself by Jesus Christ, and hath given to us the ministry of reconciliation; to wit, that God was in Christ, reconciling the world unto Himself, not imputing their trespasses unto them; and hath committed unto us the word of reconciliation (2 Corinthians 5:18-19).

God is reconciling the world to Himself through Christ, and Christ has chosen to do it through *us*. Unfortunately, we as males, in general, have done an awful lot of damage and hurt to one another, to our wives, and to our children, and we need to forgive each other and ask forgiveness of those we have wronged. There can be no true integration, no true unity, either in the Church or in society until we have been reconciled.

If we are to be truly God-style men, then we must look to God's standards, God's principles, and God's morals. We must take on a style of life that will cause us to respect ourselves as children of God and show the highest degree of respect for other people, especially those closest to us. In turn, we will earn both their respect and the right to share the message of Christ with them. It has nothing to do with clothing, or ability, or with distorted ideas of masculinity, but it has everything to do with the Spirit and the heart and the mind of God shining forth in our lives.

Rise up, O men of God!
His kingdom tarries long;
Bring in the day of brotherhood
And end the night of wrong.

Lift high the cross of Christ!
Tread where His feet have trod;
As brothers of the Son of man,
Rise up, O men of God!

    —William P. Merrill

Other *Destiny Image titles* you will enjoy reading

THE GOD CHASERS (Best-selling **Destiny Image** book)
by Tommy Tenney.
There are those so hungry, so desperate for His Presence, that they become consumed with finding Him. Their longing for Him moves them to do what they would otherwise never do: Chase God. But what does it really mean to chase God? Can He be "caught"? Is there an end to the thirsting of man's soul for Him? Meet Tommy Tenney—God chaser. Join him in his search for God. Follow him as he ignores the maze of religious tradition and finds himself, not chasing God, but to his utter amazement, caught by the One he had chased.
ISBN 0-7684-2016-4

GOD CHASERS DAILY MEDITATION & PERSONAL JOURNAL
by Tommy Tenney.
ISBN 0-7684-2040-7

IN PURSUIT OF PURPOSE
by Myles Munroe.
Best-selling author Myles Munroe reveals here the key to personal fulfillment: purpose. We must pursue purpose because our fulfillment in life depends upon our becoming what we were born to be and do. *In Pursuit of Purpose* will guide you on that path to finding purpose.
ISBN 1-56043-103-2

HOW TO RAISE CHILDREN OF DESTINY
by Dr. Patricia Morgan.
This groundbreaking book highlights the intricate link between the rise of young prophets, priests, and kings in the Body of Christ as national leaders and deliverers, and the salvation of a generation.
ISBN 1-56043-134-2

Available at your local Christian bookstore.

Internet: http://www.reapernet.com

Other *Destiny Image titles* you will enjoy reading

NO MORE SOUR GRAPES
by Don Nori.
Who among us wants our children to be free from the struggles we have had to bear? Who among us wants the lives of our children to be full of victory and love for their Lord? Who among us wants the hard-earned lessons from our lives given freely to our children? All these are not only possible, they are also God's will. You can be one of those who share the excitement and joy of seeing your children step into the destiny God has for them. If you answered "yes" to these questions, the pages of this book are full of hope and help for you and others just like you.
ISBN 0-7684-2037-7

IS THERE A MAN IN THE HOUSE?
by Carlton Pearson.
With passion and eloquence Carlton Pearson calls to men in the Church to heed God's call to true biblical manhood. Our culture may be confused about man's role today, but God has never been confused—and His people shouldn't be either! This wealth of solid, Bible-based counsel will help you transform your relationships with both men and women!
ISBN 1-56043-270-5

THE FATHERLESS GENERATION
by Doug Stringer.
The young people of today have many names—generation X, the lost generation, and the "fatherless generation." With this book Doug Stringer will stir your heart and enflame your desire to reach this generation—and thus the nation—with an invitation to return to *the* Father! *The Fatherless Generation* presents the depth of the need and the hope of the solution—a relationship with Almighty God, our Father.
ISBN 1-56043-139-3

THE HIDDEN POWER OF PRAYER AND FASTING
by Mahesh Chavda.
The praying believer is the confident believer. But the fasting believer is the overcoming believer. This is the believer who changes the circumstances and the world around him. He is the one who experiences the supernatural power of the risen Lord in his everyday life. An international evangelist and the senior pastor of All Nations Church in Charlotte, North Carolina, Mahesh Chavda has seen firsthand the power of God released through a lifestyle of prayer and fasting. Here he shares from decades of personal experience and scriptural study principles and practical tips about fasting and praying. This book will inspire you to tap into God's power and change your life, your city, and your nation!
ISBN 0-7684-2017-2

Available at your local Christian bookstore.
Internet: http://www.reapernet.com